BEGINNING
MINISTRY
TOGETHER

BEGINNING MINISTRY TOGETHER

THE ALBAN HANDBOOK FOR CLERGY TRANSITIONS

ROY M. OSWALD
AND
JAMES M. HEATH
ANN W. HEATH

Foreword by Robert T. Gribbon

THE
ALBAN
INSTITUTE

Scripture quotations, unless otherwise noted, are
from the New Revised Standard Version of the
Bible, copyright © 1989, Division of Christian Education of the National Council of the Churches
of Christ in the United States of America and are
used by permission.

Library of Congress Catalog Number
2003112708

ISBN 1-56699-285-0

07 06 05 04 03 VG 1 2 3 4 5 6 7 8 9 10

CONTENTS

———

FOREWORD

WHY DO YOU NEED THIS RESOURCE for the transition between pastors that your congregation is experiencing? The short answer is that, like other aspects of life, there is much greater complexity in a transition than there was a generation ago. Just as congregational and denominational life have been changing, so conditions under which clergy live and work have changed. This resource describes and explains these changes and the increasing complexity they have produced, to help you make some sense out of your own situation. In particular, it tries to help you see God's presence in your transition, and to draw confidence and strength from it.

The first complexity is the length of the transition period. You might think you should start looking for a new pastor when the present one announces the decision to leave. The problem here is that a congregation needs time after its pastor has left when it can identify its nature and its needs for the future. This is a period of discernment for all involved: the congregation itself, the middle judicatory of the denomination, and, ultimately, the person who will become the new pastor. When congregations call a new pastor right away, they most often want someone either "exactly like" or "completely different from" the last one. Seldom is either choice the right one. Often con-

gregations are not aware of how they and their community have changed. Thus, congregations need to take time to study who they are and what sort of leadership they need. We have become aware of the increased importance of the period of time between called pastors. When that time is truncated, negative consequences have a greater chance of occurring. In *Prime Time for Renewal*,[1] William A. Yon notes that because congregations are shaped by their leaders, the time between pastorates opens space for reevaluation and change. That early Alban Institute insight led to the creation of the Interim Ministry Network. Now, trained intentional interim ministry has matured as a specialty that can give a congregation a "breathing space" and appropriate clergy leadership during a one- or two-year period of transition. Further, the use of an intentional interim can avoid what we call the "unintentional interim" phenomenon—when a new pastor is called only to leave, perhaps under pressure, soon afterwards because of unresolved issues within a congregation, which should have been dealt with in their interim period.

The sad fact is that the number of involuntary terminations of clergy has been growing. Roy Oswald estimates from his extensive experience that at least a third of calls in recent years have resulted in a troubled or unhappy match within the first year of the new pastor's tenure. A bad match can be costly to the congregation in terms of lost opportunities, lost members, and psychological pain. It can be financially devastating if it results in severance pay, new search expenses, or even lawsuits. This resource describes how clergy and congregations can avoid such disasters by ending and beginning pastorates better.

These misunderstandings occur at least partially because of changes in the ways clergy look for a new call and congregations look for a new pastor, and in the characteristics of clergy themselves. Many of our older clergy never prepared a résumé or applied for a job throughout their clerical careers. They were "called" to the ordained ministry, and from time to time "called" to another congregation on the recommendation of a bishop or a friend. The pastor might have met once with a search committee that wasn't considering any other candidates at that time.

It was pretty much assumed that any seminary-trained man (and they *were* all men) could serve any congregation. Perhaps if they were "good," they would "move up the ladder" from smaller to larger congregations. Now we have come to realize that different congregations require different leadership skills. We live in a time of greater cultural diversity, and there is a much greater diversity among congregations within each denomination. Finding the right match between clergy and congregation takes longer. Clergy candidates are subjected to much more scrutiny, and congregations are looked at more closely also.

There are also other factors affecting clergy. Clergy require relatively higher salaries than in the past and benefits packages mandated in many denominations make for even higher minimum costs for clergy compensation. Two generations ago, new clergy were relatively unencumbered and therefore able to accept calls in a wide variety of situations. Now, most seminary graduates have considerable debt and many have spouses whose employment must be considered, so their financial and other needs are different from those of seminary graduates in the past. Additionally, the majority of seminary graduates are older than in the past; your list of candidates is likely to include older pastors with spouse and children in addition to single, younger clergy. And sometimes both spouses are ordained, which limits their deployment options. Clergy home ownership, school-aged children, or aging parents may also complicate relocation. Congregations must be larger and more stable to support a full-time clergyperson, and realistic about their ability to support their clergy, even at an "entry level."

The work of calling a pastor is more complex today because the place of the church in our society has changed and is changing. There is no consensus about the role of the church or of ordained leadership within the church. Even if the way we used to do things still works, increased switching of denominations by lay people and new diversity among our membership means that often there are new lay leaders who do not know "how we always used to do it." The interim period allows a time for self-examination and assessment. Congregations can determine what they expect of their clergy and then present their expectations accurately to candidates. Likewise, clergy can share what they can offer the congregation and their expectations from it. In this way, clergy and lay leaders can reach common and workable expectations of one another.

But where is God in all this? The answer is, "right here, right now." The good news that Roy Oswald and others bring to congregations is that God is not absent when they do not have a settled pastor. Congregations are not "vacant" just because they do not have a paid, resident, religious authority. Experienced lay leaders, denominational personnel, interim pastors, and the "transition companion" described in this resource remind us that God is present while we are in transition.

This book is about the transition period between the announcement that one pastor is leaving through the time that another pastor is well settled. The essential message is not that this is an impossible time, to be survived only with a lot of expert help. Rather, the message is that, even though the task is becoming more complex, committed people can handle it. People who have been on this journey before us can help us discover the presence of God on our journey.

—ROBERT T. GRIBBON

DIOCESE OF DELAWARE BISHOP'S ASSISTANT
FOR MISSION AND MINISTRY DEVELOPMENT

Note

1.   William A. Yon, *Prime Time for Renewal: Congregations between Called Pastors* (Washington, D.C.: The Alban Institute, 1974).

PREFACE

ABOUT 25 YEARS AGO, the Alban Institute began some disciplined reflection upon clergy transitions. That early study focused mainly on how the Alban Institute might train clergy to make more effective transitions. The results of that work continue to guide clergy transitions in seminars conducted around the country; the Alban Institute has published numerous books and monographs on the subject. In the Beginning Ministry Together project, conducted on the Eastern seaboard by six Episcopal dioceses and four Lutheran synods, Alban and the project's steering committee have attempted to consolidate recent insights into pastoral transition and take this study one step further. This later study has focused on pastoral transition from the perspectives of congregations and their lay leaders, as well as the clergy involved. The team humorously talks about studying the whole sandwich and not just the filling.

The recent study takes into account several factors that were not considered in the original work on congregational transitions. First, the early Alban research did not distinguish between sizes of congregations. A single transition format was intended to fit all clergy and sizes of congregations. Since those early days, Alice Mann and others have worked on Arlin Rothauge's theory of sizes of congregations, and the Alban

Institute now has several publications related to congregational size.[1] In the present effort we wanted to make clear the differences between transitions in family-size, pastoral-size, program-size, and corporate-size congregations.

Second, we focused more in this study on the role of congregational redevelopment in a transition. The decline in membership of many congregations in mainline denominations and the need to act swiftly to halt it was a major concern of our work. In our earlier work we often counseled clergy to make no changes in their new congregations until they had spent 9 to 12 months getting to know well the people and their congregation's history. But when congregational redevelopment is a key issue in a clergy transition, the congregation may not have the luxury of beginning slowly and allowing everyone to know one another well before any significant change takes place. Some redevelopment may have to take place during the transition.

Finally, we are particularly interested in what lay leaders, especially board presidents and search committee chairs, go through during a pastoral change. How can they be better prepared to meet the challenges of a transition and not lose their commitment to their congregation in the process through burnout?

This study examined the transition of clergy and congregation in each of the four sizes of congregation—family, pastoral, program, and corporate. We assumed that transitions would be unique to each size of congregation. We spent one day with board presidents of congregations representing each of these four sizes, another with the chairs of search committees, and a third with clergy moving into congregations of each of these sizes. From this information, Roy Oswald developed the initial draft of this book.

In the following two years we applied our findings to help clergy and congregations in transition by field-testing the use of transition companions. Six Episcopal dioceses and four Lutheran synods each sent at least four persons, both clergy and lay leaders, for two days of training as transition companions. Each of these companions worked without fee in one congregation over the course of two years. They met with other companions-in-training at least four times each year to share what they had learned and seek guidance, twice or more yearly with the transition companions in their own region, and twice yearly in Lancaster, Pennsylvania, with Roy Oswald and all the others, to share their experiences and insights. Though we learned much from the interviews with clergy and lay leaders from each of the four sizes of congregation, we learned even more by this field testing of alternative ways of advising congregations during the transitional period.

We have come to recognize and appreciate the gifts and skills of lay leaders in many congregations in carrying through a successful pastoral transition. There are also many ways in which judicatories can intervene productively in congregational life at that time. We believe that no effort of theirs will have greater benefit than that of helping clergy and congregational leaders make more informed choices while beginning ministry together. Each time a congregation does a better job of ending the pastoral relationship with the departing pastor, managing its interim period productively, selecting a pastor who can meet their needs, and then helping the newly called pastor to start up effectively, its own health and the work of the gospel will have been significantly enhanced. The result we desire is the strengthening of communities of faith to help them reach out more effectively with a message of faith, hope, and love to a broken and hurting world. To God we give our thanks and praise for the opportunity to help realize this goal.

Note

1. These include: Alice Mann, *The In-Between Church: Navigating Size Transitions in Congregations* (Bethesda, Md.: The Alban Institute, 1998); Beth Ann Gaede, ed., *Size Transitions in Congregations,* Harvesting the Learnings series (Bethesda, Md.: The Alban Institute, 2001); Alice Mann, *Raising the Roof: The Pastoral-to-Program Size Transition* (Bethesda, Md.: The Alban Institute, 2001).

ACKNOWLEDGMENTS

WE WISH TO THANK in particular the six Episcopal dioceses and four synods of the Evangelical Lutheran Church in America (ELCA) that not only contributed financially to make this project possible, but also permitted their staffs to contribute their time liberally to this venture. The dioceses of Maryland and Pennsylvania took the original initiative in this effort and also contributed most liberally to finance the study and the production of this resource. The Rev. Melford (Bud) Holland and the Rev. James Ransom, former deployment officers of these two dioceses, developed the vision for this project and then invited the other denominational judicatories and the Alban Institute to join with them in this study.

Taken together, the following judicatories collectively sponsored this research, and field-tested the use of transition companions: The Episcopal dioceses of Central Pennsylvania, Delaware, Easton, Maryland, Pennsylvania, and Washington; and the Lutheran synods of Delaware/Maryland, Lower Susquehanna, Metro Washington, D.C., and Southeastern Pennsylvania. We thank the bishops of these dioceses and synods for their support of the Beginning Ministry Together project, and thank these members of their staffs who served on the steering committee: Roy Almquist, Mary Pat Ashby, John Paul Boucher, Carol M. Chamberlain, Roy R. Coffin Jr., Robert Davis, Paul C. Donecker, Guy S. Edmiston Jr., Paul M. Ferrarone, David Fisher, Robert Gribbon, Andrea Hagan, Lawrence Hand, Carol Hendrix, Donna Herr, Roland C. Hobbs, Bud (Melford E.) Holland Jr., Judith Hoyt, Ted Kapf, Gerald E. Miller, Michael W. Newman, James C. Ransom, Anne L. Reed, Judith E. Simonson, Mark C. Sullivan, Anna N. M. Waid, Oran E. Warder, James E. Wynn, and Mary Zurell.

We thank all the individuals who were trained and worked as transition companions, as well as the many lay leaders in the congregations involved in this study, who offered their time and perspective to this project. A special thanks to Ms. Donna Herr who served as project administrator. From the beginning, this project was named Beginning Ministry Together to imply that new pastor and congregation would work cooperatively at the start of a new ministry.

We also acknowledge those whose work has taken up the original Alban Institute study of pastoral transitions and moved it a step further. Over the past five years the ELCA has trained transition specialists to conduct seminars for clergy changing congregations, through the Ending Well— Starting Strong project. Roy Oswald of the Alban Institute trained leaders to conduct the seminars, and other Alban consultants monitored seminar quality through evaluation forms and telephone calls. Originally funded through a grant from Lutheran Brotherhood, the ELCA sponsored 25 seminars yearly in various regions of the country. Now that funding has been discontinued, the ELCA has financed 12 to 15 seminars annually, with an average attendance of 400-plus clergy. Leadership for the venture came from the Rev. William Behrens, Director of Leadership Development, Division for Ministry, ELCA.

We also acknowledge the work of the Cornerstone Foundation, a ministry of the Episcopal Church Foundation, in carrying this research a step further. In the Cornerstone process, each diocese built its own transition process based on training by Roy Oswald, using Alban Institute material. In the Diocese of Los Angeles, the Rev. Hartshorn Murphy, Canon for Congregational Development, implemented a clergy-in-transition model in which newly positioned clergy meet once a month for support and guidance. In that same diocese, the Rev. Thaddeus A. Bennett, Missioner for Clergy Development and Deployment, developed a special program for clergy going into dysfunctional congregations. In the Diocese of Missouri, the Rev. Richard J. Bormes, Canon to the Ordinary, has a similar program, which begins with a two-day workshop and continues with monthly meetings for clergy in transition. The Rev. V. Gene Robinson, Canon to the Ordinary, Diocese of New Hampshire, assigns a mentor to clergy in new congregations who stays with them for two years, during which time monthly meetings are held for support and learning.

This work in the Episcopal Church has resulted in a fine manual, *Fresh Start: A Resource for Clergy and Congregations in Transition*,[1] a collaborative effort of the Episcopal Church, through the Office of Ministry Development and the Church Deployment Office, and The Cornerstone Project.[2] The Rev. Melford (Bud) Holland, director of the Office for Ministry Development, has been involved in both Beginning Ministry Together and Fresh Start. His office has supplied financial support to both of these programs.

We thank those church bodies who have helped improve the Alban Institute seminars for clergy moving from one congregation to another. Their efforts have helped us offer our readers a better resource in this handbook.

Contributors

Finally, we acknowledge the following individuals who contributed information and ideas for the articles in this handbook:

RICHARD BRUESEHOFF, director for leadership support within the Division for Ministry of the ELCA, works with the network of people across the United States who provide resources and support for pastors, congregational staffs, and leaders. He previously served as a bishop's assistant and coordinated the search and call process for the Northwest Synod of Wisconsin, ELCA.

THE REV. RIP COFFIN, Episcopal Diocese of Washington, was an early practitioner of interim ministry, serving 10 churches over a 16-year period, and was involved in the start-up of the Interim Minstry Network. He is a principal of Consultants on Purpose, LLC, serving churches and other nonprofit organizations.

RICHARD M. FARRELL, associate for deployment and congregational development for the Episcopal Diocese of Central Pennsylvania, has taught at the college level and has held management positions in global employee and customer survey administration, benchmarking, logistics, and information technology. He has participated in internal assessments and led workshops on business excellence.

BOB GRIBBON, a former Alban Institute consultant, works as a judicatory staff officer for the Episcopal Diocese of Delaware. He is experienced as a deployment officer, search consultant, interim pastor, and trainer of transition companions.

ANN HEATH, a retired elementary and language arts lead teacher, is a founding member of Union-Snyder Habitat for Humanity, and has served as its president and secretary. She was also a member of her parish search committee during a pastoral transition.

JAMES HEATH, a college teacher of Latin, Greek, and Classics for 38 years, retired from Bucknell University, where he assisted the director of Bucknell University Press. A transition companion in the Episcopal Diocese of Central Pennsylvania, he served as senior warden of his parish during a pastoral transition.

ALICE MANN pastored five redeveloping congregations before becoming an Alban Institute Senior Consultant. Assisting congregations with issues of growth, planning, and spirituality, she has also authored four Alban books: *Raising the Roof, The In-Between Church, Can Our Church Live?*, and a new book on strategic planning with Gil Rendle.

DUSTY MILLER, an Episcopal layman from Mechanicsburg, Pennsylvania, is a consultant and trainer in business and industry. He has served on various committees of his church and his diocese, and on the board of Faith Alive, a nationwide lay witness ministry.

ANNE L. REED, a deacon in the Episcopal Church, served as chaplain to a search committee. Since 1991 she has worked with congregations in transition as both judicatory

staff member and individual consultant. She is presently the congregational development specialist and deployment officer for the Diocese of Western Michigan.

ROD L. REINECKE, Rector Emeritus of the Episcopal Church of the Holy Comforter, Burlington, N.C., is a founder of the North Carolina Church Consultants Network, a retired licensed marital and family therapist, and former Alban Institute Referral Network Consultant. He has consulted and trained clergy, laity, and congregations since 1970.

NARKA K. RYAN, a retired minister of the Christian Church (Disciples of Christ), is a graduate of Bethany College and Wesley Theological Seminary. Her ministry within the Disciples was primarily in the area of stewardship and finance.

WILLIAM S. RYAN, a retired parish pastor in the Christian Church (Disciples of Christ), is a graduate of Bethany College (West Virginia), Union Theological Seminary, and received a doctor of ministry from Lancaster Theological Seminary.

ALLAN S. WYSOCKI, who served two ELCA congregations in southern Pennsylvania for 36 years, is currently director of a low-income housing development corporation and a hospital chaplain. He also chairs a synod group that relates to churches in Tanzania.

Notes

1. Fresh Start Project, 266 S. Front St., Suite 204, Memphis, TN 38103. Telephone: (865) 588-0674.
2. The Cornerstone Project of the Episcopal Church Foundation, 815 Second Ave., New York, N.Y. 10017.

INTRODUCTION

How to Use This Handbook

THIS HANDBOOK IS WRITTEN for a variety of audiences. Most articles are written to serve as resources for congregational leaders (i.e., boards, transition committees, and search committees) during the transition period between the announcement of a pastoral resignation through the end of the first year of the new pastor's tenure; some of these may be of interest to clergy and laity alike. A number of articles are of primary interest to clergy at the congregation and middle judicatory level. Transition companions, those individuals in certain judicatories who are trained to serve in a consultative capacity to congregations in transition, may use this handbook as a manual for the entire transition.

The articles are arranged in three sections. The first section is meant to be used as a "how to" manual by congregational leaders during a transition period. Articles in this section describe the activities that are necessary during a pastoral search and, in addition, several other activities that may help your transition proceed more smoothly and thus be more successful. The articles are arranged in the approximate order that the activities will occur.

The second section of the handbook contains supplementary materials. Some of these articles contain more detailed treatments of certain stages of transition;

others offer sample questions for recommended interviews, and worship resources for services to close out a pastorate. Finally, a few articles are specific to situations that arise occasionally in a small number of congregations.

The third section of the handbook contains articles of special interest to clergy in transition.

The chart on the following page suggests articles that may be of particular interest to participants with different roles in the search process. Please note with the chart that the term *clergy* may include the departing pastor, the interim pastor, and the new pastor. It is expected that most articles will be of interest to judicatory staff and transition companions, so no columns are included for them.

Copyright and Reproduction Notice

Because many of these resources are used most effectively within the context in which they are presented in *Beginning Ministry Together*, we recommend that congregations purchase copies of the book for each individual in those small-group contexts. Recognizing that many congregations will want to reproduce some of these materials for use in large-group settings, the Alban Institute has made several of these resources available for free download from the Alban Web site. These resources have been formatted for easy and clear printing on 8½ by 11-inch paper and may be printed and reproduced in limited quantities for private use in the congregation without obtaining written per-

mission. For more information, go to www.alban.org/bookdetails.asp?id=1805.

For more information on reproducing resources that do not appear on the Web site, or other materials in *Beginning Ministry Together*, go to www.alban.org/permissions.asp.

How to Use This Handbook

Number	Title	Board	Transition Committee	Search Committee	Clergy	Special Situation
PATHWAY THROUGH TRANSITION						
PT 1	Structuring Meetings for Effective Committee Work		X	X	X	X
PT 2	The Governing Board in a Pastoral Transition	X				
PT 3	The Transition Committee	X	X			
PT 4	Saying Farewell to the Pastor	X	X		X	
PT 5	Meetings with Judicatory Staff	X	X			
PT 6	Holding Exit Conversations	X	X			
PT 7	Interim Pastoral Services	X	X		X	
PT 8	The Search Committee	X		X		
PT 9	The Congregation Profile	X	X	X		
PT 10	Identifying What to Look For in a New Pastor	X	X	X		
PT 11	Maintaining Confidentiality	X	X	X		
PT 12	Developing a Pool of Candidates			X		
PT 13	Tracking Information about Candidates			X		
PT 14	Communicating with Candidates			X		
PT 15	Talking with Candidates			X		
PT 16	Working toward a Final List of Candidates			X		
PT 17	Making Background Checks			X		
PT 18	Candidate Visits to the Congregation	X	X	X		
PT 19	Working out a Contract with the New Pastor	X			X	
PT 20	Welcoming the New Pastor	X	X		X	
PT 21	Telling Your Pastor about the Congregation's History	X	X		X	
PT 22	Discovering the Congregation's Norms	X	X		X	
PT 23	Evaluating the Ministry of Pastor and Congregation	X	X		X	

Number	Title	Board	Transition Committee	Search Committee	Clergy	Special Situation
ENRICHING TRANSITION						
ET 1	Making the Most of the Interim Period	X	X		X	
ET 2	The Role of Transition Companion	X	X	X	X	
ET 3	Leadership Changes During and After a Pastoral Transition	X	X		X	
ET 4	Transition in Multi-Congregation Linkages		X		X	X
ET 5	When the Departing Pastor Stays in Town	X			X	X
ET 6	Sample Questions for Exit Conversations	X	X		X	
ET 7	Survey Questions for a Congregation Profile	X	X	X		
ET 8	Questions for Reflection on the Transition Process	X	X	X		
ET 9	A Ritual for Ending a Pastorate	X	X		X	
ET 10	A Service for Ending a Pastoral Relationship	X	X		X	
CLERGY EXPERIENCING TRANSITION						
CT 1	Surviving a Farewell				X	
CT 2	Coping with the Stress of Transition				X	
CT 3	Transitions for Clergy Spouses		X		X	
CT 4	Forming a Pastor/Parish Relations Committee	X	X		X	
CT 5	Discovering the Psychological Contracts of Members	X	X		X	
CT 6	The "Honeymoon Period" of a New Pastorate	X	X		X	
CT 7	Preparing to Make Changes				X	
CT 8	Power Analysis of a Congregation				X	
CT 9	Starting Up as a Redevelopment Pastor				X	X

PART 1

PATHWAY THROUGH TRANSITION

Structuring Meetings for Effective Committee Work

One of the most notable challenges during the transition period is the increased number of meetings held in the congregation. Members of the board are suddenly responsible for many things that the pastor has done; they may need to meet more often. The search committee, and possibly a transition committee, is appointed; much of their work is accomplished during meetings. Not all people enjoy going to meetings, but most are willing to do so when the meetings have a clear purpose and when the group works productively and, for the most part, harmoniously. There are a few basic things that committees can do to optimize their time together, and by doing so to help prevent people from burning out because of the additional responsibility and time requirements that have been placed on them.

Spiritual Grounding

For all church meetings, it is important for the group to maintain a spiritual focus as they work together. Every meeting should begin with some type of devotions that will help participants turn their attention from their busy lives and toward God. A committee that seeks to be open to the guidance of the Holy Spirit must take the time for spiritual grounding. Whether a committee appoints a chaplain or members take turns leading devotions, this is an activity that should never be overlooked.

Team Building Strengthens Trust

It is important for people who are working together—particularly on a search committee—to be able to express themselves frankly, even when it means introducing some controversy into the group. But to be able to do this, a level of trust must exist between committee members. The first step is for people to get to know one another; people who know one another often have a greater level of trust.

Conscious scheduling of team-building activities can help people get to know one another and thus for trust to develop, particularly when committee members have not previously worked together. Team-building activities usually give people a chance to share something simple about themselves; for example, how their day or week has gone. In addition to building trust, this sharing helps people feel cared for—cared for enough to be willing to listen to others' concerns.

Following the opening devotions, the committee chair can pose a simple team-building question, and ask members to respond with a sentence or two. Since members of a group can occasionally get caught up in their own responses, it may be helpful for the chair to suggest a time limit for each person's sharing. Here are some examples of questions that can be used for team building before the meeting's agenda begins:

- In a sentence or two, what was the high point and the low point of your day (or week)?
- Who are the people for whom you felt like weeping this week?
- Which people seem to have the Spirit of God working through them?
- If you could change one thing about this congregation, what would it be?
- What do you like most about serving on this committee? What concerns you about this committee?
- Where have you seen the hand of God at work today?

A different set of team-building activities can be based on a short Bible reading. This passage could be the same one used in devotions, if the worship leader has not already presented a reflection on it. The selected passage is read aloud, and a short period of silence is observed. Then each member of the group is asked to respond to one of the following:

- Name the character with whom you identify.
- Tell how you think the passage relates to our task.
- Imagine that you could get into conversation with *(name of character in passage)*. What question would you like to ask her or him?
- If *(name of character in passage)* were asked to give a piece of advice to this group, what do you think she or he would say?

Although these activities may take only about 15 minutes, there may be individuals who want to skip team building early in the group's life together and get to the committee's work right away. But in the long run, the time spent on team building may be some of the most productive time the committee spends. As trust develops among committee members, group creativity may

thrive; creative solutions emerge best when people are comfortable expressing opinions without feeling that they will offend someone. When group members trust one another, they are willing to fight hard for their views and not feel hurt if different views prevail. When committee members have come to know a little bit about one another, individual differences become apparent and, at the same time, an acknowledgment and appreciation of the different gifts that each committee member possesses can emerge. When committee members become aware of the talents possessed by others, they may listen more carefully and respectfully.

Reflection on Process

A third activity that leads to more productive meetings is to allow 10 to 15 minutes at the end of every meeting for committee members to reflect on "how we worked together today." The chair can see that each member has an opportunity, in turn, to say what she liked about the way the group worked together, and what concerned her about the meeting. Productive meetings always have a goal in mind when the meeting ends. An evaluation period can assist them in reflecting on how well they accomplished their task. The results of this assessment can be useful in planning future meetings and in helping a group recognize ways it works together most effectively.

Time Well Spent

These three simple additions to meetings—spiritual grounding, team building, and attention to process—probably take about half an hour of the committee's time at each meeting. But the time they take will pay off in the long run. When the group's members have been spiritually focused, have come to trust in one another, and have taken the time to reflect on the way they work together at each meeting, they should be able to function more efficiently and, as a result, more effectively.

PT 2

THE GOVERNING BOARD IN A PASTORAL TRANSITION

THE PASTOR'S ANNOUNCEMENT of departure or retirement poses a set of challenges to a governing board, as well as to the congregation as a whole. During the transition, the board will have to function as both managers (seeing that the day-to-day affairs of the congregation continue to run smoothly and effectively) and leaders (developing a vision for the future, working to present it to people so they understand it, and motivating them to work toward a vision they agree is viable and necessary). In addition to their regular responsibilities as members of the board, the board must also deal with the many changes that are occurring in the congregation. They must assume responsibility for tasks that the pastor has taken care of or arranged for. They must decide on what kind of interim pastoral services are needed, and what goals, if any, should be accomplished during the interim period (see PT 7; ET 1). They have to provide direction throughout the discernment and search process. And later, they will have to develop a good working relationship with a new pastor. What specific responsibilities must they assume, how can they prepare themselves for their task, and what resources are available for dealing with the unfamiliar situation?

Many people are more accustomed to management than to leadership, and different board members may work more effec-

tively in one arena than the other. As a first step, it may be helpful to divide the board's responsibilities into clusters to help determine the skills that are needed for each:

- Taking over behind-the-scenes tasks.
- Looking after the welfare of the congregation in the interim period.
- Helping define the congregation that a new pastor will minister to.
- Managing the discernment and search process, including exit and start-up phases.
- Attending to the board's spiritual and organizational needs in the absence of a pastor.

Taking Over Behind-the-Scenes Tasks

The board needs to make sure its members know what tasks the pastor did routinely and make arrangements to see that they are done. The scope of these tasks will probably be greatest in congregations that have a small or part-time secretarial or administrative staff. As suggested in the resource section (see ET 6), the pastor should be asked during the exit conference if he has made a list of such responsibilities. If the list has not been completed, a member of the board should ask to sit down with the pastor and work on the list together. After the pastor leaves, the board will have to assume or delegate these responsibilities.

Looking After the Welfare of the Congregation in the Interim Period

The pastor has been in a position to know what is going on in peoples' lives: who are sick, bereaved, or facing personal or family crises. The pastor has also looked ahead to upcoming events: church seasons and holidays with their related events and celebrations, community plans that involve the congregation, visits of judicatory staff. The board must provide for congregational planning and support of members. If the congregation has arranged for interim pastoral services, much will depend on the contract that has been developed. A full-time interim pastor will be able to perform many of the same member support, planning, and worship activities that the pastor has performed. A part-time interim pastor will be able to do less, and weekly supply pastors will probably not be involved at all in these functions; in this case, lay participation must be developed for both member visitation during times of illness and crisis, and planning for church events.

A transition committee can also help coordinate the life of the congregation and give oversight to the many changes taking place as a called pastor leaves. They will need to be in close contact with congregational members to monitor how this transition is affecting them personally (see PT 3).

Helping Define the Congregation That a New Pastor Will Minister To

A congregation's identity and vision may depend to a great extent on the leadership of its pastor. In a time of transition a governing board may concentrate on managerial functions and neglect the need to provide focus and vision for the congregation. A carefully selected interim pastor, intentional or not, can help maintain existing focus and programs. But the board must play a greater role in looking for opportunities to discover new ventures that reflect the congregation's identity and interests. The interim pastor can sup-

port these efforts in liturgy and pastoral activity, but the board's initiative is essential.

If only supply clergy are available in the interim period, the board will have to assume, or delegate to others, the leadership roles for activities that at least maintain the identity of the congregation. Candidates for the position of pastor will notice the efforts of a congregation that is concerned about its vitality and growth during a transition, when it might be all too easy to lose the impetus for change, waiting instead for a new pastor to do the work for them.

Managing the Discernment and Search Process, Including Exit and Start-Up Phases

As the elected governing body of the congregation, the board has ultimate responsibility for all aspects of the transition, even when many activities are shared with or handed over to other groups (such as transition and search committees). Thus the board should monitor, by regular contact, the managerial functions that have been delegated to other groups. The functions (which are addressed throughout this handbook) include:

- Graciously accepting the departing pastor's notice of resignation or retirement.
- Arranging closure and farewell events for the departing pastor and family, including involvement of congregants.
- Contracting and working with an interim pastor or those who provide pastoral services; closing out this service at the end of the interim pastorate.
- Appointing a search committee and, possibly, a transition committee.
- Deciding on the desirability of engaging a transition companion and, if one is decided on, contracting for services.
- Arranging for action on search committee recommendations and contracting for terms of service with the chosen pastor.
- Welcoming the new pastor and family.
- Starting up the new pastorate (including, e.g., welcoming and installation

events, setting up mutual ministry committee).

In addition to these expected responsibilities, circumstances may call for the board to take a more proactive role; for example:

* Establishing a new relationship with the judicatory: the transition will entail its closer involvement with the congregation.
* Attending to the morale and dynamics of the congregation in the course of the transition and being alert to signs that suggest the need for an intentional interim pastor, even if one was not initially selected.
* Considering ways the congregation might be made more attractive to candidates for pastor (e.g., by making improvements to the property).
* Facilitating the continuation and even expansion of lay ministries within the congregation and outreach activities in the community.
* Ensuring financial stability and even expanding the congregation's financial resources.
* Challenging the congregation to become even more vital and active during the interim period, not merely by keeping activities in the congregation going, but also by looking for ways for the congregation to expand activities and attract new members in the interim period.
* Looking for opportunities for spiritual enrichment in the transition process itself, encouraging members to view all life's transitions as opportunities for spiritual growth.

Attending to the Board's Spiritual and Organizational Needs in the Absence of a Pastor

The departure of the pastor may deprive the board of a vital ingredient: a chaplain, an organizing force for spiritual nourishment, and provider of pastoral care. The transition period will place heavy responsibilities on the board, ones that will only increase the need for these services. In the absence of a pastor, the board must provide these services for itself or arrange for care from someone else.

If the pastor has prepared the agenda for and chaired board meetings, the board president will have to assume these functions. A small executive committee, if one does not already exist, could be formed for this purpose. The president, with this committee, will have to arrange discussion of the agenda for board meetings with committee chairs.

If board members have not played a role in devotions at board meetings, a range of options is possible. One or more members could be asked to lead devotions. Alternatively, a non-board member of the congregation might be asked to serve as the board's chaplain during the transition.

The board may have looked to their pastor to provide pastoral care in other ways (e.g., by organizing and leading board retreats). Even if this form of pastoral care has not taken place in the past, now is the time for the board to attend to it, given the additional stress that the transition is likely to produce. There may be a retired clergy member in the community who could be asked to provide such pastoral care (for an appropriate fee), or members of the congregation might be called upon.

The transition period is thus a time for the board to become much more conscious of the challenges that the absence of a pastor leads to. But there are opportunities for growth in the congregation as well: the board is in a position to call upon the talents and concern of members of the congregation. The congregation can thus be enabled to gain a sense of participating fully in the affairs of the transition. A congregation can begin a process of transformation in this way and can become more attractive to a suitable new pastor while building the foundation for an effective new pastorate.

Resources for Boards

If the board follows the suggestions of the last section, it will discover resources in itself to meet some of its new challenges. Other resources are available in the congregation and outside:

- The congregation can be asked to pray for the board and others working during the transition.
- The transition committee can plan and oversee many activities related to the transition.
- Members can be called upon to assist in planning and carrying out transition activities (e.g., farewell celebrations, contributing to the development of the profile, helping with welcoming functions).
- The judicatory executive and staff can be called on for information and advice on specific questions and can be asked to request the support and prayer of other congregations in the judicatory.

- A transition companion, if one is available, can offer valuable advice and support, and may provide a wider perspective on the transition than that of people within the congregation.

Conclusion

A board that stays on top of a transition by the means described here will realize several benefits:

- It will encourage and strengthen the congregation.
- It will strengthen itself.
- It will attract the best candidates for pastor: people who are looking for a congregation that wants to share ministry, rather than expecting the pastor to "do it all."
- It will help the congregation to rediscover itself and its faith in responding to the needs of the board and to the absence of a permanent pastor.

PT 3

THE TRANSITION COMMITTEE

MANY CONGREGATIONS ARE UNFAMILIAR with what happens when a pastor resigns or retires. Some members of the congregation may react with sadness, anger, and even fear at the loss of the pastor; others may be energized by the possibility of renewing the congregation in some particular directions. The governing board is likely to be distracted by the need to run the congregation and assume some of the pastor's functions. Some individual or group needs to concern itself with the whole transition process; the board may wish to delegate this responsibility to another group.

A congregation goes through three phases in a pastoral transition:

1. Termination and exit of the departing pastor.
2. Discernment, search, and call for the new pastor, which coincides with a period of interim ministry. Some congregations call an interim pastor and see to it that the interim has a solid contract for what is to occur during this interim period.
3. Contracting with a new pastor and start-up of the new pastor.

Groups in the congregation such as the search committee and governing board will have authority to handle specific tasks during the transition, but someone should be charged with becoming familiar with and monitoring the whole of it. All parts of the congregation are likely to be affected by the transition. It will be a great help if there are a few people to whom individuals and groups can turn for information and support and who will be expected to watch for things that are not being taken care of during the transition.

Functions and Composition of a Transition Committee

The transition committee is an ad hoc committee with the responsibility of (1) becoming informed on any and all aspects of the transition, both those specific to the congregation and those that apply to most congregations of their size and type; and (2) advising those in authority in the congregation of actions they should take to facilitate the steps of the transition. Appointment of a transition committee is one of the board's first tasks after the pastor's announcement of departure.

The committee should be small: its membership may run from three to six or more, only if the right kind of people are available and willing to serve. Members should have these qualities:

- considerable life experience
- some experience in pastoral transitions
- spiritual depth

9

Transition committee members should know the congregation well and be widely respected in it, and have sufficient free time to be on call when emergencies or critical decisions call for their assistance. In small congregations, the entire board or a few of its members can serve effectively as a transition committee, but they must be clear about the demands of the dual role.

The specific concerns of each of the three phases are set out in "How to Use This Handbook" at the beginning of this book. If the congregation has arranged for the services of a transition companion, that person will be expected to work closely with the transition committee, helping it to understand its role and to communicate its findings and recommendations to those concerned with them or authorized to act on them. The following is an overview of the most important things the transition committee needs to be sure are done in each phase of the transition.

Termination and Exit (See PT 4; ET 6)

- Close effectively with the departing pastor: work with both pastor and congregation.
- Arrange exit interview for departing pastor.

Discernment, Search, Interim Pastor (See PT 7; PT 8)

- Examine alternatives and arrange for pastoral care and worship leadership.
- If interim pastor is to be engaged, advise on contracting.

- If intentional interim pastor is called, advise on tasks.
- Set up search committee and advise it on procedures and self-care strategies for its members.
- See that the congregation is made aware of general progress in the search and that its needs in the transition are met.
- Serve as a resource for the interim pastor.

Contracting and Start-Up (See PT 18 through PT 21; CT 4)

- Advise search committee and board on contracting procedure.
- Advise on welcome of new pastor and family to both congregation and community.
- Be available as a resource for the new pastor for the first year of start-up.

Conclusion

Congregations become aware of the complexity of a pastoral transition only after they have gone through one. The insight gained by a transition committee can form an important resource for the congregation, as well as the judicatory. The selection of a new pastor and start-up of a new ministry can both be facilitated by a conscientious transition committee. Recognition of this committee's work as it is dissolved at the end of the transition will mark the end of the start-up period and signal that the new ministry has become established.

SAYING FAREWELL TO THE PASTOR

THE PERIOD OF PASTORAL TRANSITION begins with the announcement that the pastor will be leaving and extends through the end of the first year of the new pastor's ministry. The length of time between announcement and actual departure is variable: a retiring pastor may announce that intention as much as a year ahead; a pastor who accepts a new call may depart a few weeks to a few months later; in rare situations, catastrophic illness or sudden death may create an immediate vacancy.

In the seminar "Finishing Strong, Ending Well," which is geared to clergy who have served a congregation for 10 years or more, we advise having the pastor announce his or her intention to retire four to five years ahead of time. This allows both the pastor and the congregation to do some strategic planning for what important goals the congregation wants this pastor to complete before leaving. We often recommend the pastor have a three-month sabbatical to prepare for these last four or five years so that the pastorate "finishes strong." Time should be built in to "end well," such as setting aside the last six months of the pastorate for closure. But in every circumstance, it is always important for the congregation to say farewell and to end the pastoral relationship in such a way that both are prepared and enabled to move on to new relationships and opportunities.

The departing pastor usually announces the intention to leave to the congregation's governing board first, asking them to keep this information confidential until the news can be shared with the entire congregation. It is important to let everyone else in the congregation know at the same time; this announcement is best made by a letter that is sent to every household. A letter is preferred to an announcement at Sunday worship services, because some of the congregation's members will likely be absent. After the letter has been sent, both pastor and board should plan opportunities for formal leave-taking.

The number and scheduling of farewell events depends in large part on the length of time between announcement and departure but may also depend on the pastor's length of tenure in the congregation. When a pastor retires after many years of service, the congregation may want to schedule several events to offer as many people as possible the opportunity for a public farewell to the pastor. It is important, too, to recognize and give thanks to members of the pastor's household. The congregation or the pastor may also wish to include appropriate individuals from the community in some events. Whether a few or many, these events can take a variety of forms, depending on the resources and interests of the congregation, such as:

- a potluck supper followed by skits or a "roast" that expresses the congregation's affection for the pastor;
- a picnic which might include singing, square dancing, or games;
- an extended coffee hour;
- an invitation to the middle judicatory executive to preach at worship and then make informal comments and a presentation at a coffee hour or luncheon following the service;
- a "this is your life" evening;
- a musical evening or special art show.

If the congregation wishes to give a gift to a departing pastor, it might be presented at a final event when many members of the congregation are expected to be present. For clergy who have been serving the congregation for 15 years or more, all of the above can be used during the final six months, holding one event each month.

In cases where the pastor will continue to live in the same community, it is especially important that the *pastoral* relationship with the congregation end, even though ties of friendship will continue to link the pastor to many people. In this case the board may decide to draft a formal agreement with the pastor that outlines the pastor's future involvement in the congregation. (See ET 5, which outlines the length of time a departing pastor agrees to stay away from the congregation before returning as a worshiping member.) In addition, the congregation may wish to emphasize and celebrate the end of the pastoral relationship with a liturgy designed for that purpose (see ET 9; ET 10).

In addition to public leave-taking events, the board or its officers may encourage the pastor to make time for private good-byes. When possible, the pastor should meet with various parish groups, as well as with individuals, to reflect on their ministry together. Depending on the amount of time available, individual meetings can include both personal visits and phone calls. It is important that pastor and members of the congregation have an opportunity not only to say thank you to one another, but also to express regrets and move past differences, reaching a point that will allow both to move into new relationships more easily (see CT 1).

The congregation and its officers should be aware that the process of departing and saying farewell is different from the pastor's point of view. The pastor has to balance the emotional, personal effects of the departure with the many pastoral responsibilities that the departure brings. The pastor must focus on both saying farewell properly and leaving the affairs of the congregation in good order. As some clergy are deeply feeling types, they may have difficulty closing well with individuals and groups. It is appropriate to ask about the departing pastor's closure plan and about ways the congregation can support doing this well. When it is not done well, a congregation is often left feeling wounded, unable to move on with life with the new pastor. Lay leaders should meet with the pastor to be sure they know how and where to locate records and important information on the running of the congregation, and are aware of details that the pastor has routinely handled. Having a written list of such information will ensure that necessary information is preserved through the transition period.

And finally, while contacts with the judicatory must be made as soon as the pastor's departure has been announced and some plans for initial interim pastoral services must be made, the congregation should not begin to prepare its profile or hold discernment events until the pastor has departed. If an intentional interim pastor is needed (see PT 7), the congregation may also want to wait to decide what particular tasks that person will be contracted to perform. Deferring these activities until the pastor has departed allows the congregation to focus on ending the pastoral relationship well and also to develop a sense of itself as a congregation without the pastor who was part of its identity. After the pastor leaves, the congregation can get a better sense of where it is and where it wants to go in the future.

The interim period offers a time for congregational self-reflection and planning. This work should focus on future needs and not be tied to the years past.

Though there is an understandable desire on the part of many congregations to move ahead quickly, allowing some time to pass before entering into the search process will, ultimately, allow the congregation to know itself and its needs for the future, and to find a new pastor with whom the congregation can fulfill its ministry.

PT 5

MEETINGS WITH JUDICATORY STAFF

SOON AFTER THE ANNOUNCEMENT of the pastor's retirement or resignation, the congregation's governing board should arrange a meeting with a staff member from the denomination's middle judicatory. That body's staff members have worked with many congregations in transition and can be a valuable resource. They can explain the requirements of your denomination and the expectations the judicatory executive may have, as well as outlining the resources they can offer to your congregation. In addition, they can also offer guidance on procedures that other congregations of your size have found effective in their search processes.

Meeting with the Board

Before the meeting takes place, the board president and judicatory staff member can discuss the meeting's agenda by phone, therefore allowing an opportunity to ensure their concerns will be addressed. If time permits, members of the board may also read "How to Use This Handbook," which offers an introduction to many aspects of the search process, and may alert the board to the need for discussing particular items.

Specific items to discuss with the judicatory (usually in more than one meeting) might include the following.

Saying Farewell to the Pastor

The judicatory can advise about ways of saying good-bye, and may also be able to offer particular help in situations when the pastor's departure is abrupt, when relationships have been poor, or when the departing pastor will continue to live in the community. In these cases, outside intervention may help heal hurt feelings and forestall problems in the future (see PT 4).

Interim Pastoral Services

The judicatory may have specific recommendations about the kind of services that your congregation requires. If the previous pastor has had a long incumbency, is leaving after a traumatic event, or the relationship has been contentious, a long-term intentional interim pastor may be recommended—to allow the congregation time to learn more about itself and its needs for the future and perhaps to go through a healing process. The judicatory may suggest specific interim clergy for your congregation, and can also provide guidelines for contracting with them (see PT 7).

The Transition Period

The staff member can give suggestions to help this period go smoothly. She can help you decide whether you need a separate transition committee and whether the participation of a transition companion is available and would be helpful, and also give some guidance on how long the process may take and what expenses the congregation will face. She can also discuss how the transition time can be used for congregational growth and development. The judicatory may also recommend clergy or lay leaders in other congregations who have had a recent transition advise for when judicatory staff members are not available (see PT 3; ET 2).

The Search Process

The staff member can point out things to consider when selecting a search committee, such as size, representation of a variety of viewpoints, and selection of a chair. She may also make suggestions about this committee's relationship with the board (see PT 8).

The judicatory staff member can discuss the steps that usually occur in a search process. She can explain specifics, such as procedures for advertising vacancies, in denominations that follow that practice. The judicatory staff member will also explain how names are submitted, indications of interest are channeled, prescreening (if any) is conducted. She or he can also discuss strategies for maintaining confidentiality by both governing board and search committee, while keeping the congregation informed about progress of the search process (see PT 11; PT 12).

The Search Committee

Often, a member of the judicatory staff will also meet with the search committee. Along with issues raised above, the search committee may also be concerned about the following.

Keeping God in the Process

The staff member can suggest effective ways of practicing prayer and discernment dur-

ing the search process. She or he can tell how other congregations have used a committee chaplain or how members of a committee have shared this responsibility.

The Congregation Self-Study

Some judicatories require a self-study and have developed questionnaires and other tools for gathering information, which the staff member can discuss. If the congregation wishes to focus its attention on certain areas of emphasis, the staff member may suggest ways to do so effectively. The staff member can also offer advice for using the self-study to develop both a congregation profile (to be sent to interested candidates) and a profile of the kind of pastor needed (to narrow the list of applicants). (See PT 9 and 10.)

Specifics about the Search Process

As the search proceeds, your judicatory contact person can provide information about ways to learn about candidates in conversations with them, how to perform background checks and check references, the manner in which a call is offered to the selected candidate, and the negotiation of a contract. (See PT 15, 17, and 19.)

Self-Care for Committee Members

The search committee's work will extend over a period of many months. The judicatory representative may be able to suggest ways to develop a process that will acknowledge and utilize the gifts of all committee members, and ways of dealing with conflict or burnout. She or he may be able to offer names of consultants who could be called upon if necessary (see PT 1).

On Your Way

Any meeting will yield a number of action items: committee appointments, telephone contacts, and so on. Someone should be designated to keep a careful list of these items, make sure someone has agreed to do each item by a specified date, and then be certain that everything gets done.

The topics that have been introduced will help you get started on your search process. Remember that the transition period will be a learning process, and you will think of many more questions of your own.

Answers to many of your questions will be found throughout this handbook. These answers will help prepare you to take the best advantage of outside resources, such as judicatory staff or a transition companion.

Note

This article is based in part on material written by H. I. "Dusty" Miller. Used by permission.

HOLDING EXIT CONVERSATIONS

THE DEPARTURE OF A PASTOR offers an opportunity for information-gathering conversations in which the pastor and governing board can separately comment on the pastorate that is ending. Such conversations can help both pastor and congregation to end the pastoral relationship productively and to adapt more readily to the futures that await each.

The exit interview that businesses conduct when an employee moves to another position (inside or outside the company) or retires might appear to be a model for information gathering. But that model is unsatisfactory in certain respects for the departure of a pastor. Businesses try to learn about an individual's job or a work group's functioning so that the employee hired to replace the person leaving can be trained or directed to work more effectively for the company's overall benefit. A member of the personnel office (someone possibly not known to the employee) will probably conduct the interview, and the interviewer may not be particularly concerned with the employee's future welfare.

In a congregational setting, information gathered from a departing pastor and from board members as a pastor prepares to depart can help the congregation understand itself better, can provide guidance to those involved in the transition that is beginning and the search for a new pastor that will follow, and can help the departing pastor to take the appropriate steps to close out the present pastorate and prepare for the challenges that the future will bring. Thus the term *interview* seems inappropriate: *conference* or *conversation* better suits the context in which information will be gathered.

Matters to consider in holding these conversations include:

- Who should lead a conversation?
- With what preparation and in what setting should the conversation be held?
- What information should be sought?
- How should a conversation be recorded and transcribed?
- What happens to the records of the conversation?

Who Should Lead a Conversation?

The person guiding the conversation should have some experience in leading such conversations, and must be someone the pastor can trust and in whom the board has confidence. An outsider offers the best opportunity for gathering useful and unbiased information—a staff member of the middle judicatory, a transition companion, or a trusted clergyperson from a nearby congregation could be asked to serve. As a last resort, a member of the pastor's congregation might have to be called upon, though it should be recognized that an insider might feel constrained about introducing sensitive or controversial topics. Likewise, the pastor or board members may not feel comfortable making comments to a member of the congregation that someone could take personally.

With What Preparation and in What Setting Should the Conversation Be Held?

The person who is to lead the conversations should lay the groundwork with both pastor and board, describing to each the nature and purposes of the conversation. If the pastor agrees to participate, the question of tape recording the conversation should be discussed. Keep in mind that a tape recorder is less intrusive to a conversation than note-taking, but if a recorder is used the pastor must have the right to edit the transcript of the conversation. The board conversation should also be taped and members given the opportunity to edit their remarks for clarity and accuracy.

The setting should be as informal as possible. The principal questions and topics to be addressed should have been agreed upon earlier by the leader, pastor, and board president, and a list of them prepared. For the sake of comparisons later, the questions addressed in the two conversations should be as similar as possible. The sample questions in ET 6 offer a start for the leader to approach issues and information that will be of most benefit.

The aim of these preparations is to identify topics on which participants can reflect. These reflections could facilitate the pastor's adjustment to future work or retirement, the work that the search committee will undertake, and the start-up of a new ministry in the congregation. The reflections may also contain matters of interest to the middle judicatory. From a well-led conversation, a coherent picture of the congregation and of the pastorate that is

ending can emerge. A free-flowing conversation skillfully guided will generate more useful insights than short answers to factual questions.

What Information Should Be Sought?

The topics should address the pastor's ministry, developments in the congregation throughout it, and current conditions and concerns in the congregation. The conversation should also try to touch upon the pastor's situation at this time in her life, matters that may relate to the transition, and matters of interest and importance in the congregation's history. Different information on similar topics may emerge from pastor and board, according to the aims and perspectives of these participants.

The pastor can be helped in this conversation to close out the ministry well and to understand the adjustments that may be needed in a new situation. The pastor may be able to offer insights, warnings, and encouragements that will assist the search process. More generally, the congregation can benefit from the historical perspective of the pastor. This perspective has value in itself as a record of a pastorate that can form part of the congregation's archives.

Given the number of people involved in the board's conversation, the conversation leader will have to focus carefully on larger issues and draw the conversation away from excessive concentration on minor, peripheral, or less productive topics.

How Should a Conversation Be Recorded and Transcribed?

Under the best circumstances, the conversations will be recorded on tape and arrangements will have to be made for their transcription into written form. This will entail a cost if a suitable volunteer cannot be found; the transcriber must be someone who can be trusted with confidential matters. If written notes are taken, the person taking notes should prepare the draft. The pastor will receive a copy of the transcript to edit; while the pastor should have the right to remove statements he would not like to become public, the leader should encourage the pastor to limit changes as much as possible so that the transcript remains an accurate account of the conversation. The conversation leader may suggest that explanatory material (e.g., full names, dates) be added, in square brackets, with the pastor's approval. Members of the board should be given a copy of the transcript of their conversation and a similar opportunity to make simple corrections or clarifications.

What Happens to the Records of the Conversations?

Once final versions of the conversations are available, the board should control their use, ensuring that the pastor has a copy of her conversation. The board needs to decide what information from them, if any, will be presented to the congregation, search committee, middle judicatory, or new pastor. The edited transcripts should be preserved in a confidential file, and decisions made on the disposal of tapes, notes, and unedited transcripts. The board should compare the perspectives presented in the two conversations. Finally, the board should convey to the departing pastor its thanks for participating in the conversation and for the information and assistance the board has received from it.

Conclusion

At the end of a pastorate, the pastor and board members may welcome the opportunity to place some thoughts about the ministry that is ending on a permanent record. Doing so in a planned manner can be an important component in saying farewell. Exit conversations of pastor and board, carefully structured and led to focus on important concerns, can both provide a form of letting go of the ministry that is ending and bring to light information and ideas that can guide pastor and congregation as each enters a new phase of life.

INTERIM PASTORAL SERVICES

EVERY CONGREGATION will want to arrange for someone to lead worship and provide pastoral care when the congregation is between pastors. Planning for interim pastoral services should begin during the exiting phase of the departing pastor's ministry, but the work of the interim pastor should begin only after the departing pastor's ministry has officially ended.

There are three basic types of interim ministry. Ranging from least to most complex, they are:

1. supply ministry
2. simple interim ministry
3. intentional interim ministry

Supply clergy agree to conduct regular or special services and to perform specified pastoral services (e.g., visiting those who are sick or are grieving) for remuneration on performing each function. There is no expectation that a supply pastor will do any more than the services to which he has agreed.

Simple interim ministry entails contracting with the governing board for a specified time period (e.g., six months, with the possibility of extension by mutual agreement) to perform most of the functions of the regular pastor: conduct services, provide pastoral care, and meet with the board as well as other congregational committees and groups. Simple interim ministry as-

sumes that the regular functioning of the congregation will continue largely without change. Such a simple interim can be either part time or full time.

Intentional interim ministry goes far beyond simple interim ministry. An intentional interim pastor has special skills to help a congregation address identified concerns. To be sure, all the problems of a congregation will not be solved during a 9- to 18-month interim period, and most long-term problems will also need to be addressed by a new pastor. However, when there are difficult issues that would seriously hinder a new pastor's ability to gain the trust and confidence of the members of the congregation, it is better to have an interim pastor deal with them. Intentional interim pastors have received specialized training to handle this task, and some make a career of serving in intentional ministries.

An intentional interim should be your choice if your congregation has concerns related to:

- the ending of a long pastorate (more than 10 years);
- the difficult ending of a pastorate (the previous pastor may have died, been pressured to resign, or been guilty of some malfeasance);
- antiquated systems of governance;
- the need for staff changes;

- chronic financial problems or serious financial irregularities;
- deferred maintenance;
- congregational volunteers who hold decision-making positions but have done nothing of significance for some time;
- significant change in the congregation or its neighborhood, or ministries that are not serving the congregation and the surrounding community;
- clear-cut divisions in the congregation;
- the desire to explore more extensively the possibilities for significant change (e.g., growth in numbers, a new approach to stewardship) before a new pastor is in place;
- possible merger or linkage with another congregation.

In the event that a congregation cannot find or afford a full-time interim pastor, it might decide to work with two people. One would provide simple interim ministry, and the other would consult with those charged with leading the self-study and other transitional work. This latter person might be a trained transition companion; that is, someone who can assist the congregation in conducting an audit of its ministry to ascertain whether significant changes need to take place before a new pastor arrives. Another alternative might be to contract with a part-time interim to conduct worship and manage transition issues and leave noncrisis pastoral care and management issues up to lay leaders.

The decision about what kind of interim services are needed should be made after consideration of the needs and on the advice of the middle judicatory, whose staff members may be helpful in suggesting or locating individuals for the congregation.

Contracting with the Interim Pastor

It is important for both congregation and pastor to know what is being expected during an interim period. In cases where the congregation has a sense that there are problems but cannot identify them precisely, it may be wise to contract for more

hours in the first three months of the interim. This will allow the pastor extra time to meet with leaders and other key members of the congregation to get a fuller version of the congregation's story. In these three months, the interim should identify tasks that she and the congregation, working together, can accomplish in 18 to 24 months.

Issues to be addressed during the interim period can also be identified from the exit interview of the departing pastor. A well-conducted interview will reveal things the departing pastor intended to accomplish but had to relinquish as the pastorate drew to a close, the departing pastor's perception of key challenges facing the congregation, or things the departing pastor knew should have been done but were neglected (see PT 6; ET 6). Other concerns for the interim period can be identified through the self-study process (see PT 9; ET 7) or a governing board retreat. After specific concerns are identified, the congregation and interim pastor may want to modify the contract to include certain tasks and set out responsibilities of both interim pastor and the congregation. Periodic review of progress on these tasks and other responsibilities should be provided for in the contract.

In addition to the specific concerns the interim is expected to address (if any), the contract should also include information about hours of work (part or full time), salary, pension, health benefits, continuing education time, as well as provision for denominational meetings or other responsibilities. The interim should get vacation (for example, a week each quarter) that can either be accumulated or used along the way, and the policy for weekly days off should be stated. Finally, the contract should state clearly that the interim cannot be considered as a candidate for a permanent position in the congregation.

Evaluation in the Interim Period

Evaluation determines the extent to which the purposes, goals, and objectives of the ministry of interim pastor and congregation have been met. Evaluation provides an opportunity to discover how and why actions taken did or did not meet those intended goals, and it allows the congregation and interim pastor to think about further actions. During evaluation near the end of the interim period, the congregation can think about matters the new pastor should attend to, and the interim pastor can reflect on more effective ways to serve future congregations.

Why the Interim Must Never Be a Candidate

For reasons that follow, the Interim Ministry Network believes that an interim pastor should never be a candidate in the search:

- A person who has served as an interim may have an unfair advantage over other candidates, because she is already known and liked by some members of the congregation. In the event that the interim is not the final choice for pastor, advocates of the interim may become alienated, and the interim pastor's effectiveness for the remainder of her work may be jeopardized.
- At the same time, an interim pastor may have people who do not like him or who may be oppositional from the beginning of a permanent ministry, but who do not voice their dislike with the assumption that the interim is here only for a short term.
- If denominations were to allow interims to become candidates, it would destroy the concept of interim ministry. Other clergy might think that interim ministry is a way to test out congregations to see if they are interested in serving them permanently.
- Because other clergy would know that

ministerial ethics had been violated when the interim accepted a call, relationships with fellow clergy could be damaged.
- An interim pastor's style of leadership may not be acceptable or appropriate for members of a congregation in a permanent relationship.
- The relationship of a congregation to an interim is sometimes based on its vulnerability during the transition; the need of members for guidance could lead to inappropriately influenced decisions.[1]

Thus, interim contracts must prevent consideration for a call as permanent pastor of a denomination, and denominational executives must uphold these provisions.

Closing Well with the Interim Pastor

An exit conversation with the interim pastor, which can follow the format of the pastor's exit conversation, may produce insights that will be of value to the new pastor. If certain tasks were not accomplished, the interim can explain the factors that prevented them. The interim can share her perception of the congregation's strengths and what she hopes they can accomplish in the future. The interim may also offer to answer any questions the new pastor has.

One of the greatest gifts an interim pastor and congregation can give each other is to say farewell effectively. The interim's departure mirrors the departure of the pastor in many ways, and the interim and congregation will go through many of the same activities they did when saying farewell to their pastor. Together, the interim pastor and congregation can reflect on and rejoice about their time together, and say farewell in a way that allows both to move into new relationships.

Note

1. Based on guidelines from the Interim Ministry Network, Baltimore, in Roger S. Nicholson, ed., *Temporary Shepherds: A Congregational Handbook for Interim Ministry* (Bethesda, Md.: The Alban Institute, 1998).

THE SEARCH COMMITTEE

THE SEARCH COMMITTEE undertakes a spiritual journey on behalf of the congregation as they work to identify the person who will become the next pastor. Far from being a group of "head hunters," the search committee is entrusted with the task of finding the next spiritual leader for its congregation. The future mission and ministry of the congregation are going to be deeply impacted by the choice made by this committee.

Selecting the Committee

The way a search committee is selected varies among congregations. In some congregations, the board (or its chair) may simply appoint a committee. In other congregations, a number of individuals may volunteer or be nominated, and the committee may be elected from the list of candidates by the board or by the congregation as a whole. The size of the committee may also vary among congregations. Some middle judicatories strongly recommend a committee of a certain size; sometimes a congregation's bylaws stipulate the composition of the committee. If no specific size has been dictated, the board must be sure that the number chosen is large enough that no one is overburdened, and yet small enough to allow meaningful participation for every committee member, maintain confidentiality, and keep its expenses (particularly those involved with travel to distant locations to visit candidates) within the congregation's budget. The best size for a decision-making group is seven (plus or minus two).

A number of characteristics are important for members of a search committee. Those who select the committee should seek members who are:

- diverse, representing the various constituencies within the congregation;
- endowed with a variety of skills for the committee's tasks;
- rooted in the history of the congregation, with an understanding of its future direction, based on the congregation's mission, vision statements, and self-study;
- widely respected;
- able to maintain confidentiality;
- able to commit a great deal of time throughout the search process (at least a year);
- good listeners;
- flexible and experienced in working well in a group;
- known to keep commitments and follow through on assignments.

It is important to remember that the search committee not only represents the aspirations of the congregation in the discernment process with candidates, but also presents and represents the congregation to candidates during their meetings.

The search committee needs a chair who has good communication skills and the ability to lead a complex group. That leader must be able to pay attention to internal dynamics to ensure that personal differences are acknowledged and dealt with directly, while keeping the group moving through the search process. The chair will also have to be in regular contact with the board, the judicatory, and the transition companion, if there is one, and maintain communication with the congregation by making regular progress reports. In addition, the chair should be in contact with candidates as the search progresses, keeping them informed of where the committee is in its process, and letting them know if the committee eliminates them from active consideration.

It is important for the search committee to be clear about the specific tasks they are to perform, and about their mandate for identifying final candidates. The search committee needs to know if it is responsible for conducting the self-study and preparing the congregation's profile. The committee must also understand whether they are being asked to present a small number of finalists for board consideration, perhaps prioritizing them, or whether they are expected to identify and recommend one candidate for a board or congregational vote.

Early Meetings

In the early meetings of the committee, it may be helpful for each member to share his vision for the congregation and new pastor. It is important for the committee to discuss and appreciate the spiritual process of discernment they will undertake with the candidates. If members do not know one another, the committee may decide to engage in some team-building activities (see PT 1). The committee should also set

ground rules for its overall functioning, including set times for committee meetings to begin and end as well as procedures that ensure that all opinions can be expressed in discussions. Committee members should also be absolutely clear what maintaining confidentiality means; for example, can they go home from meetings and debrief with their spouse (see PT 11)? In these early meetings, the committee may be divided into subcommittees for such functions as preparing the congregational profile, identifying the attributes to be sought in a pastor (based on the profile), and developing questions to be used when talking with candidates (see PT 9; PT 10; PT 14).

The committee should also discuss its procedures for reaching decisions. The committee may decide to make decisions by consensus; that is, to continue discussion until reaching a position the whole committee can accept. The committee may also agree to make major decisions on the basis of a large majority (e.g., 75 to 80 percent) if consensus cannot be attained.

Maintaining a Spiritual Focus

The committee might also choose a chaplain whose leadership in worship and prayer will help them maintain a spiritual focus. This chaplain need not be a member of the committee, but should attend all meetings, observing the committee's process and communication, and helping the committee work through any difficult moments. A chaplain or other nonmember observer, such as a transition companion, is able to maintain a valuable outside perspective on the committee's work and can comment on the state of the committee and recommend alternate ways of working when needed. This person might also lead the group to reflect at the end of each meeting, helping each of them to identify the progress they have made and to reflect on their own participation in the process. A chaplain can also ask the committee to pause for silent or corporate prayer at times when the process is breaking down. Throughout the process, a chaplain can call the congregation to prayer for the search, the search committee, and candidates. Alternatively, members of the committee can take turns serving as chaplain, leading opening and closing prayers, and serving as a process person at meetings for which they serve as chaplain. A process person is one who pays more attention to the way decisions are made than in the decisions themselves. Process has to do with how members listen and react to one another, whether the committee is dominated by certain people, and whether the concerns of all members are heard and taken seriously.

Caring for Committee Members

Recognizing that the search process is a demanding one, it is important to pay attention to the support and self-care needs of each search committee member. There are several things that committees can agree to do at the outset.

The committee can agree to show concern and respect for people's personal lives by beginning and ending all meetings on time. They can agree that they will use meeting time efficiently by keeping on task—this is easier to do with the use of a meeting facilitator such as a transition companion or a chaplain who is not a member of the committee. The committee should pledge itself to follow the procedures it has adopted to ensure that each member has an opportunity for input into every discussion (e.g., by agreeing that every member will be able to present his or her comments before a general discussion begins).

Further, the committee should take the time to debrief at the end of every meeting, so that concerns about the group's workings are shared regularly. Such debriefing can be as simple as asking each member to offer a word or phrase indicating what they are taking home with them from the meeting, or to describe how pleased they are with the way they worked together at the

meeting. Note that a debriefing is not a time for debate, but rather for each member to make observations about the group's process skills. These observations can help the chair or facilitator to take note of issues or practices that detract from the group's functioning and to help the group figure out how to make future meetings more productive.

From time to time, the committee may benefit from having refreshments at a meeting, holding the meeting in another setting, or taking time for committee members to know one another better. Some members are likely to interact informally at or between meetings, to discuss issues that concern them, and thus to go beyond the team-building activities that took place at early meetings. Others, however, may need to be drawn into such interaction by a few minutes of informal discussion at the start of a meeting.

Committee members must resist the urge to "push" the process or try to rush through or omit necessary steps. And, finally, the committee should be reassured that it is acceptable not to choose one of the candidates; starting the process again is much better than calling someone who is not well suited for the congregation.

Congregational Support for the Committee

As the search process begins, it is important for the congregation to identify and recognize the members of the committee in a brief liturgical ritual during Sunday worship. This is an opportunity to begin the habit of corporate prayer for the discernment process and also to ask for prayer support for the search committee. Some congregations have found that homebound members appreciate the opportunity to participate in the search process through their prayers. Members of the congregation can be reminded through the newsletter to pray not only for the work of the search committee, but also for the members and staff who are keeping the congregation going, the departing pastor and family as they begin a new chapter in their lives, and especially for the candidates.

Ending the Search Process

The search committee will spend many hours on behalf of the congregation, and it is important, when their job is complete, to acknowledge their work formally. Again, the committee might be recognized during worship, and should be publicly thanked by the congregation. It is helpful for committee members to get together in some sort of exit activity in which they reflect on the work they have done and their own participation in it. They should also bring together and destroy the personal information they have about all candidates and the search process. In addition, the committee should have a celebratory event, possibly a dinner with the new pastor, and give thanks for the opportunity for service to the congregation, the ties they have made with one another, and the work that God has helped them through.

PT 9

The Congregation Profile

EARLY IN THE SEARCH PROCESS, a congregation profile must be developed. This profile should be a thorough and accurate description of the congregation's people, programs, financial resources, and facilities. The profile will help the board and search committee to identify characteristics to look for in a new pastor. In addition, because it will be sent to potential candidates, it will usually create the first impression of and serve as an introduction to the congregation; for this reason, the finished profile should appear attractive and positive. A profile should help the congregation see itself accurately, and inspire outsiders to want to know the congregation better. Since the identity of a congregation is influenced by its relationship with its pastor and changes once a pastor has left, it is preferable that the profile be developed only after the pastor has departed.

Information for the profile can be gathered in a variety of ways: from survey questions, conversations about programs, home meetings, or a weekend retreat. It can also be extracted from existing records such as directories, official registers, and board minutes. The following sections describe activities that elicit member input.

Survey Questions

Many judicatories spell out very specifically the kind of self-study information congrega-

tions should collect about themselves. Often, the judicatory will provide a questionnaire to the congregation; since broad participation leads to a more realistic description, the board should decide how to administer it so that the greatest number of people has the opportunity to participate. If the congregation must develop its own questionnaire without direction from the judicatory, it can use the questions found in the supplementary section (see ET 7). Another source of possible questions is the "Congregational Health Survey" found in the appendix of the book *Discerning Your Congregation's Future.*[1] Any questionnaire used should include information that can be analyzed to determine age ranges of members and their children; numbers of years members have been in the congregation, denomination, or community; percentages of membership by gender, marital status, and educational background; and residential patterns. The questionnaires should also enable members of the congregation to state preferences about clergy characteristics, worship, programs, and congregational needs.

Answers to survey questions can be in written form. (For example, a questionnaire can be completed on a Sunday morning before, during, or immediately after worship services. In this instance, opportunities to fill out the questionnaire at other times can be provided for those who were absent on that particular day, but who want to participate.)

These questions can also be answered in an open-space activity that might follow a potluck meal. In this situation, the corners of a large empty room are designated as "A," "B," "C," "D" (the letters that indicate different answers to questions); if space allows, one or two areas in the center of the room can also be identified by letter to allow for more response choices. As each question is asked, participants move to the area of the room that corresponds to the response they have chosen. In order for the collected data to be useful, it is necessary to appoint individuals to keep careful counts of the numbers that move to each area for every question.

Conversations about Programs

Over the years, a congregation may develop effective ongoing programs and areas of special emphasis; in some cases, a pastor's interests and leadership have contributed to or diminished development of such programs. The departure of the pastor offers the opportunity for examination of the congregation's programs and special areas of interest, both present and past, to help people identify program priorities.

A large group can be divided into smaller groups for conversation. After about 30 minutes of discussion, each group can report on its findings to the whole group. Following a break, the small groups can meet again to develop two lists: (a) the strengths of the congregation we want to build upon and (b) the areas where we should grow and develop. These lists can be shared with the whole group, and then collated by the group that is preparing the profile.

Home Meetings

Groups of about five to nine (but not larger than twelve) gather in homes. Someone from the search or profile committee should chair each meeting. Two possible formats for discussion are suggested.

In the first format, each group considers two questions: (1) What do we like about our congregation as a spiritual community? (2) What concerns us about ourselves as a spiritual community? (Some congregations may choose to use a term that is more familiar than "spiritual community.")

As an alternative, each group can undertake a Bible study based on the first three chapters of the Book of Revelation. After oral reading of the letters sent to seven churches, the leader should point out that in the first part of each letter, God commends the church for certain things; in the second part of the letter God says "But this I have against you." Each attendee should then be asked to make two lists: one of things God might commend the congregation for, and the other of things God might have against the congregation. After about 20 minutes, the lists should be shared aloud. The similarities and differences can be discussed, and two lists that represent the greatest consensus of the total group should be prepared. The final lists from either format should be forwarded to the search committee.

A Weekend Retreat

A weekend retreat allows the assembled group an extended period for reflection and conversation about the congregation. If a wide spectrum of people can attend, it can be very valuable. The group can have several periods of Bible study and prayer, followed by small group discussions about the history of the congregation, where it seems to be, and where it should be heading. As points of clarity emerge, a facilitator can write them on newsprint, with a summary produced at the end.

Developing Information into the Profile

When these activities have been concluded, and descriptive information has been gathered, the congregational profile can be developed. Some data can be presented in general terms to give an overview of the congregation (e.g., over 20 percent of our members are retired; 60 percent of those who completed the questionnaire are women; 65 percent of the children in the church are in elementary school), but other information should be presented in more detailed form. Those who read the profile should be able to learn membership numbers, staff (including which positions are filled by volunteers), current worship attendance, schedule, and preferences (e.g., traditional or contemporary). They would also appreciate information about spiritual life in the congregation, as evidenced by Bible study and prayer groups, mission focus, and events that foster fellowship and community life. In addition, important linkages with other congregations or groups in the community should be mentioned. The facilities of the church should be described completely, including its worship seating capacity, public rooms, education rooms, and the congregation's and pastor's office space. Any housing the congregation provides for its pastor should be adequately described. In addition, major problems in or recent improvements to the physical plant should be noted. It is also important to include any information that shows how the congregation is unique, and to highlight programs or features that will make potential candidates interested in knowing more.

The completed profile should also include a short history of the congregation, its committee structure, congregational goals, and a copy of the current budget. Photos of groups, activities, and buildings are well worth including, and if color photos are used, printing costs can be contained by keeping them all on a page or two which can be inserted by hand. In addition, information about the congregation's community and the neighborhood surrounding the church might be provided. Many congregations are now including Website addresses for organizations and points of interest in the community.

If a congregation is located in a neighborhood that has undergone significant change over the years, the board and search committee may want to gather demographic data about that area. Companies that specialize in providing demographic data, with summaries of factors a congregation should consider as it seeks to relate to its neighborhood, have menus of the kinds of information they can provide.[2] In many cases, denominations or judicatories have already subscribed to such companies, and congregations can obtain data from them at reduced cost.

Final Preparation of the Profile

The board, and possibly a small group from the congregation, should review a draft of the profile. Attention to graphics and proofreading are important in preparing the final draft, so it is attractive to readers. It is wise to ask someone in the judicatory office to review the final draft, even if judicatory approval is not required. The board should decide how many copies of the profile are needed within the congregation (e.g., for board, staff, search committee, availability to members of the congregation), in addition to those that will be sent to candidates.

Developing an accurate profile can be challenging, but those who participate will gain an understanding of the congregation they might not have had before. New insights that emerge can be referred to the board for their consideration, and can be part of any future strategic visioning. Most important, a well-done profile can present the congregation to candidates in a way that encourages them to apply and makes them want to learn more.

Notes

1. Roy M. Oswald and Robert E. Friedrich Jr., *Discerning Your Congregation's Future: A Strategic and Spiritual Approach* (Bethesda, Md.: The Alban Institute, 1996).
2. Two such companies are Percept (800-442-6277; www.percept.info) and Visions/Decisions (800-524-1445; www.visions-decisions.com).

PT 10

Identifying What to Look For in a New Pastor

BEFORE THE SEARCH COMMITTEE considers any applications, it must have a clear idea of the characteristics and skills the congregation needs in its new pastor. These characteristics and skills will be incorporated into a pastor description by which all candidates will be measured. Some of these characteristics will have emerged during the development of the congregation profile. Others, however, can be identified on the basis of the congregation's size.

Learning from the Congregation Profile

If members were asked during the development of the profile to reflect on the most successful aspects of the ministry of former pastors, a good sense of the qualities and skills of an effective pastor in that congregation should have emerged. In addition, if the congregation survey has asked members to identify areas of congregational life they think a new pastor should emphasize, the specific personal or professional qualities needed to work in these areas can be pinpointed.

The demographic information resulting from the surveys may also help identify desirable skills for a new pastor. For example, a congregation found to have a large number of teenagers or homebound adults will doubtless seek a pastor experienced in working with them.

The search committee must evaluate all these sources of information and come up with a core group of characteristics or skills it will look for as the committee gets to know the candidates. Realizing that no candidate may be a perfect match for all of the desired characteristics, the committee may have to develop and prioritize a primary list of most desired characteristics and a secondary list of other desirable characteristics. The committee might group the desired characteristics in particular areas (e.g., liturgy, education, outreach) and rank the areas in importance as well as skills within an area. For example, the committee might rank liturgy as the most important area but rank preaching above skills in liturgical music.

Characteristics Based on Congregation Size

In addition to pastoral characteristics that have been identified in the profile process, specific pastoral and organizational skills are needed in congregations of different sizes. Those who study congregations have found that they fall into four general categories based on their average Sunday attendance. Although the numbers that define the size categories vary, the following breakdown, based on average Sunday worship attendance, has proven useful: family (50 or fewer); pastoral (50–150); program (150–350); and corporate (350 +). The characteristics of each size of congregation and the clergy skills needed for each are identified as follows:

Family-Size Congregations

These congregations are sometimes called patriarchal or matriarchal congregations because a few strong members are their real leaders; clergy are often peripheral to the ongoing life of the congregation. These congregations are often yoked (so that two or three together can pool financial resources to come up with a minimum salary) and frequently have high clergy turnover. This turnover of clergy makes it difficult for these congregations to engage in long-term planning or to accomplish long-term goals.

Family-size congregations benefit when they find clergy who are willing to stay with them for a long time. This may be possible if a congregation can find a bivocational pastor who will serve for 15 to 20 hours per week while holding a weekday job. Because that person already has another job, source of income, and housing, she may be willing to serve for a longer period of time. Alternatively, some denominations allow congregations to identify persons to be trained and ordained as lay pastors. A lay pastor, possibly along with other individuals called to ministries of administration, education, and outreach, can provide leadership for a family-size congregation.

Pastoral-Size Congregations

In these congregations, the pastor is involved and dominant in almost every function of the congregation. Members of the congregation have close fellowship bonds, and the pastor has close contact and relationships with many members.

These congregations need a pastor with strong interpersonal skills. Search committee members may ask themselves, "Is this a person I want calling on me when I have trouble?" In this size congregation, the pastor serves as an attraction for newcomers, builds relationships with members, and facilitates fellowship in the congregation. A pastor here must be able to work well with people of all ages. In addition, because the congregation may not be able to afford adequate administrative help, the pastor must have some organizational abilities.

Program-Size Congregations

This size of congregation has a larger range of programs to meet the various needs of its members. The pastor is not directly involved in many of the programs; the programs are run by volunteers from the congregation. The pastor interacts with these program leaders and affirms their work but does not have in-depth relationships with many members.

While good interpersonal skills are needed in a program-size pastor, they will be used with a smaller group of people. This pastor must have the ability to develop leadership skills in others and to train other people to do specific ministries such as visitation, youth work, and running the Christian education program.

Corporate-Size Congregations

A congregation of this size has several paid staff members who oversee its programs. Lay volunteers may not hold many positions of leadership. Because a congregation of this size is likely to be diverse, the staff must reflect that diversity, for example, in age, gender, theology, personal style, and race or ethnicity.

The pastor of such a congregation is challenged first by the need to lead a diverse staff to work well together. Most corporate-size congregations expect their pastor to be a superior preacher and worship leader, and to work well with excellent musicians. Usually, successful pastors in these congregations have been trained as part of a large staff in other corporate-size congregations.

Characteristics and Skills for a Congregation Changing Size

Search committees should be aware that pastors who have experience only in congregations of one size may not be effective in a congregation of another size. In addition, they should realize that if their congregation is approaching the upper size limit of one of these categories and wants to grow larger, they should call a pastor who has skills to function well in the larger-size congregation. This person may well have characteristics and skills that are different from those of their former pastors.

Conclusion: Developing and Using the Ministry Description

When the congregation identifies the skills and characteristics needed in a new pastor, the search committee can prioritize and identify a core of "must have" skills and characteristics for a new pastor. These skills and characteristics can be included in the profile and in any advertisements for the position. More important, the list of desired skills and characteristics can be used as a foundation for the questions that will be asked of candidates and also as a standard against which to judge the answers the committee receives.

PT 11

MAINTAINING CONFIDENTIALITY

MANY PEOPLE ENJOY "BEING IN THE KNOW," being the first to learn a piece of news as an insider, even if they do not intend to pass it on to others. But sometimes it is hard to resist the temptation to tell others about something, even when the news may be harmful or derogatory to someone. Everyone must be reminded of this human tendency when the search process begins, and those who select the committee should look for candidates who are known to demonstrate discretion. The need for confidentiality should be reiterated to committee members after they are selected for the search committee and throughout the search process. Search committee members must be reminded that the trusted friends with whom they might share information could also be friends or relatives of candidates or their references. In fact, it will be most helpful if the entire congregation is well prepared from the beginning to accept the need for confidentiality and to feel offended at any breach of the principle during the search process.

All information about candidates must remain strictly within the search committee. Spouses, board members, other members of the congregation, even the interim pastor and people outside the congregation may be eager to learn the names of candidates or information about them such as age, gender, location, experience, and interests. This is all confidential information that should not be shared outside the committee. From the time the congregation begins to receive candidates' names and information about them, the confidentiality policy should be reasserted and the commitment of all search committee members to observing it secured.

In addition, search committee members must respect and protect the right of each member to express their opinions and observations freely. Conversations within the committee about candidates, goings on in the congregation, and other pertinent matters must be kept as confidential as the information about the candidates themselves. Search committee members can be candid with one another only if they are certain that their comments will not be shared outside of the committee. For example, if a committee member expresses reservations about the individual who is finally selected as pastor and this information is made public, the relationship between these two individuals, and even the pastor's ability to enter the congregation without controversy, could be compromised.

Search committee members must learn to distinguish information and decisions about candidates from general information on the search process. Still, it is probably best to agree that only the committee chair will comment publicly on the search, in writing and orally. The chair should report, at Sunday services and in the newsletter, what the committee is doing: for example, preparing the congregation profile and defining the characteristics and talents the committee will look for in a new pastor; processing the first list of candidates it receives, and developing a list of people to investigate more deeply; conducting phone interviews; seeking background information; preparing for site visits to candidates' home congregations; arranging for one or more finalists to be brought for a visit.

Members of the search committee—in fact, all members of the congregation—should be alert to the spreading of information that should be kept confidential. Anyone who hears such information should notify the search committee chair, who should then try to stop the spread of such information by identifying its source (if possible) and asking the person or persons involved to act more responsibly. If it turns out that a baseless rumor is being spread, measures can be taken to end its circulation. If a search committee member is the source of a leak, the committee should discuss how to proceed; that is, whether the seriousness of the matter suggests the offender be dropped from committee membership.

In the case of a serious breach of confidentiality, the search committee chair will also have to notify the judicatory executive of what occurred and discuss how to proceed. If the chair fails to do this, the transition companion or, ultimately, any concerned participant in the search should take this step.

A final means of maintaining confidentiality in the search process is for every member to return to the chair or destroy all information they have received about candidates, together with any notes they have made during the search process. Some committees plan to have paper shredders or a bonfire at their closing celebration; others ask members to destroy materials in private. Having the material destroyed will help ensure that the confidentiality, which the congregation has worked so hard to maintain, will be preserved.

In the end, the highest praise a search committee can receive is the comment, "I never knew any details of the search, and now I'm happy to meet the new pastor without any preconceptions."

PT 12

DEVELOPING A POOL OF CANDIDATES

THE GOVERNING BOARD OR SEARCH COMMITTEE has produced a congregation profile that gives an accurate description of the congregation, its current condition, and its aspirations. This document will be a major element in creating candidate interest in what the congregation both has to offer and needs. There has also been developed—largely from the profile and the congregation surveys that led up to it—a ministry profile, or criteria by which the search committee will assess the suitability of candidates for the position of pastor as it gets to know them through application dossiers and interviews. But how does a congregation move into the next phase of its search for a pastor? How does it develop a pool of candidates from whom it can begin the process of selection?

The ways of developing a pool of candidates for a congregation vary widely. This is a significant point in which denominations and judicatories differ in their management of pastoral searches. Some congregations are given no role in developing candidate pools; others work with few or no restrictions and conduct their search entirely as they see fit. Given this variation, congregations should understand clearly what their denomination and middle judicatory expect the congregational role to be in developing a pool of candidates. This article deals with situations in which a congregation has some leeway and responsibility in forming this pool and suggests ways to attract the greatest number of suitable candidates.

Congregations that have no role or only a limited one in developing a pool of candidates can still use other articles in this handbook to help evaluate candidates who have been presented to them. Congregations that are assigned a pastor with no input from the congregation can learn from other articles how best to terminate the relationship with the outgoing pastor and help the new pastor begin in the congregation.

Congregations that do have discretion in selecting a pool of candidates perform this task using three principal techniques: reviewing denominational or judicatory registries, obtaining names of candidates by word of mouth, and advertising in denominational or wider circulation periodicals. The first method is the most important and effective; the others are supplements to it.

Denominations that have a national registry, such as the Episcopal Church, usually have the middle judicatory serve as intermediary between the searching congregation and the national registry. The judicatory wants to ensure that the congregation's description of itself reflects the congregation accurately and positively and that the criteria for a pastor that have been identified reflect its needs. When a candidate from outside the area is an applicant, members of the judicatory staff may be helpful in checking references through conversations with their counterparts in the candidate's home area. In some cases, a judicatory executive can act unilaterally to bar a candidate from a search pool, or advise a congregation of a potential problem.

For reasons such as these, many judicatories are the first to receive applications from candidates. These bodies may then present to the congregation either a limited set of names from the list of applicants, or the entire list of names, along with comments on them. The executive may also add to the list of formal applicants names of candidates from within the judicatory who are known to be interested in a move and who seem suitable candidates for a particular search. The pool of candidates need not be considered closed at this point. Two means exist for supplementing it.

First, names of candidates may be received by word of mouth: from current members of the congregation, former members who have maintained contact with the congregation, or other clergy. Names of clergy who have not applied through the formal process that are received in this way may be added to the pool when certain formalities have been observed. These formalities should include consultation with the judicatory executive, who may know of reasons for advising against approaching certain individuals. Individuals whom the judicatory approves should be approached by the chair of the search committee by letter or telephone and asked if they are interested in being considered as candidates. If any of these possible candidates are inter-

ested in proceeding further, the committee chair sees that they receive the materials that the formal applicants have received, and can ask them to provide the same kinds of information that other candidates have provided.

Second, positions may be advertised in denomination periodicals or religious journals of wider circulation. The purpose of such advertising is primarily to attract the attention of clergy who may not be listed in the formal national registry of the denomination, but who may be interested in a particular congregation for a special reason. For example, they may have special reasons for wanting to live in the area, or the congregation may have a unique feature that appeals to their own interests such as an active music program, or a need for a pastor familiar with sign language. Such advertising should be used to highlight a unique feature of a congregation and to supplement the regular process of forming a pool of candidates.

When the pool of candidates has been constituted, the process of evaluation and selection can proceed. Note that a search committee will sometimes discover that no candidate in a pool matches the congregation's criteria, or that those who do lose interest in the position. The search committee should not be discouraged at this point. It is possible that they have not fully described their congregation or adequately identified the criteria for their next pastor. With courage, faith, and a renewed commitment to a successful search, a new and different pool of candidates can be constituted. A congregation that reexamines itself under such circumstances can both become stronger and a more attractive option for the right pastor.

PT 13

TRACKING INFORMATION ABOUT CANDIDATES

AS THE SEARCH FOR A NEW PASTOR PROCEEDS, the search committee will receive a variety of forms of information on candidates; in particular, from application forms, interviews, and references. The quantity of information may become oppressive and, in the case of interviews, not all members of the search committee will receive the data at firsthand, if they miss an interview for some reason.

It is important, therefore, for the search committee to develop methods for recording and processing information before the search process begins. By doing this, the committee will be sure that data is available for use when it is needed. A person with experience in office procedures for handling data can be an invaluable resource. A file should be established for each candidate, listing the categories of information received, the evaluations individual committee members make of information in each category, and the consensus the committee reaches as a whole on each candidate in each category. The aim is twofold: to preserve a formal record of fleeting impressions before they fade away, and to develop a basis for comparing candidates by measuring them against the criteria the search committee agrees to adopt.

One exception to creating a file for each candidate does exist: when the committee reviews the initial information about candidates, it may be clear that certain candidates do not meet the committee's criteria in any meaningful way. These candidates may be dropped from consideration immediately without a file being established for them. Through this action, however, a new policy becomes necessary: the regular notification of candidates of the progress of the search and their standing in it (see PT 14).

Processing Information

The different sources of information require different kinds of processing; the initial applications will vary according to denomination or judicatory practices. The committee should develop categories it is interested in for recording basic information. These may include such things as: length and type(s) of pastoral experience; preferences expressed or inferable as to liturgy, theology, and type of congregation; expected salary. Information on some things the search committee is interested in may not be available or inferable: age, gender, marital status, ethnic identity. While denomination practices in such matters vary, most attempt to open their ministry to all qualified persons and to discourage selection on the basis of factors they consider irrelevant to an effective pastorate. Search committees are best advised to concentrate on the essential features of a pastor who will serve the congregation well, and not look at factors that may serve as a basis for irrational prejudice.

It is important to look carefully at material that allows a candidate some free expression: personal statements, write-ups in newspapers or periodicals, authenticated statements from identifiable sources. Try to get a sense from this material of a candidate's style and character: does a spiritual depth come through? a sense of humor? a sense of attention to detail? openness and willingness to be known? Or do you see stuffiness? self-centeredness? something that just doesn't seem right?

Interviews and conversations offer a different source of information. Another article describes how to arrange and conduct a telephone interview or conversation, devising appropriate questions for candidates to respond to and requests for them to talk about their specific experiences in situations that parallel your criteria (see PT 15). Each member of the committee should have an evaluation sheet prepared for making notes on every conversation and recording impressions and an assessment of each candidate in terms of specific criteria. After the conversation and the writing of these assessments, committee members should each express their individual reactions to the candidate (with no discussion), and then the entire group should discuss what to record as a result of the interview, noting areas of general committee agreement, as well as important minority reactions. It is important that all members of the group be allowed to express their views without feeling pressured by time, the convenience of others, or the self-assertiveness of dominating members. A neutral observer, such as a transition companion or committee chaplain, can play an important role in empowering all evaluators at this critical point in a search process.

Maintaining Objectivity

The value of recording information is most evident when all the interviews have been structured to be as similar in format and questions asked as possible. It is possible for candidates to attempt to distinguish themselves and to affect the evaluations of an interview consciously or unconsciously by the image they project. Evaluating groups must be on their guard against losing objectivity and distance when dealing with a possibly manipulative person, who somehow takes control of a conversation from the evaluators. It may be possible to maintain the sense of objectivity, but if the interviewee retains control, measures should be in place to deal with the situation following the interview. Here are some suggestions.

1. A process person (e.g., chaplain or transition companion) could alert the committee to the change of focus and suggest a disciplined discussion of the possibility of skewed impressions.
2. In the process evaluation that should conclude all sessions, include discussion of a candidate's attempts to sidetrack an interview.
3. Include on the interview rating form a question or two on a candidate's handling of the interview.
4. Allow a period of time (a few days) to elapse and then have the committee review its findings. Encourage those whose views may have changed or solidified to discuss an interview in greater depth.
5. Engage in a period of prayer before and after evaluating candidates.

Careful Tracking Pays Off

In the recording and reuse of data involving the group's consensus formed from the impressions of individual members, if it is performed with care, regularity, and consistency, the committee will find itself educating itself throughout the search process on what their congregation's needs really are and what candidate can best meet them. A lot of work will have been done by the time the new pastor has been selected, but the search committee will have a sound basis for justifying their selection to themselves and to the governing board or congregation, depending on the denomination's procedures.

It is ironic that all this work will go into the shredder or fire at the conclusion of the search. But if the work of recording and tracking search data has been performed correctly, the result will repay its loss: the confidence of search committee members and of their congregation that the search has been disciplined, fair, and spiritually satisfying.

PT 14

COMMUNICATING WITH CANDIDATES

AT EVERY POINT in an ethical search process, search committees will respect candidates and give them as much information as possible—without either misleading or being dishonest with them. All candidates should have a clear idea of where the search committee is in its deliberation process and of their status as candidates. Many search committees develop the practice of keeping candidates under active consideration as long as they can; such a committee feels that a candidate whose assets attract even one member very strongly merits further consideration and longer inclusion of the candidate in the committee's discernment. On the other hand, when it is clear that a candidate has definitely been removed from further consideration, it is not fair to string him along with false hope. Thus the search committee should agree upon procedures to keep candidates informed of their status in a search at the beginning of the discernment process, and should follow these procedures closely until a final decision is made. Such procedures might include:

- An initial, personal note of thanks (these are hand-written by some congregations) for participating in the search. The note should also indicate the period of time (not more than three weeks) by which the committee will be back in touch.
- Applicants who are dropped from consideration at any time should receive a note stating that the committee has decided not to go forward with their candidacy and offering best wishes for their continuing ministry. The reasons for this decision should not be stated, but the committee chair should be prepared to follow up by phone with any candidate who asks for clarification. For candidates who are eliminated from consideration during the first review of materials, this information can be combined with the note of thanks for participation.
- Every few weeks, candidates who are still under consideration should receive a personal note with a brief update (e.g., we will be having phone conversations during the next three weeks; we are in the process of checking references). Each communication with candidates should indicate clearly when the committee will next be in touch, and the committee must be sure to honor the promised schedule (even if the next communication only tells candidates that there has been a delay in completing a certain activity). After phone conversations, the committee

may decide to assign responsibility for ongoing written communication to one of the telephone interviewers, since the interviewers are now more familiar to the candidate than other committee members.

- When the decision for the call has been made, other final candidates should not be informed until the letter of agreement with the selected candidate has been signed by all required individuals (candidate, board president, and judicatory officer). All who know the name of the chosen candidate should be reminded that the call is not official until the formalities are concluded, and that this information is still confidential. The notification to unsuccessful candidates of the congregation's decision to call another final candidate should be made by phone, followed by a letter.

Congregations should check with their judicatory to see whether other procedures are recommended, including having their written communications checked by a lawyer.

Wise committee members will always remember that no matter how well they think they can control who knows what about their work, information has a way of leaking and often gets passed on. As committees deliberate about how to deal with candidates, members should ask themselves, "Would we want all our candidates to know that this is what we are saying or doing?" and "Do I want to be associated with a congregation that treats people this way?" If the answer to either questions is no, the committee needs to plan to proceed in a better way.

TALKING WITH CANDIDATES

IN THE COURSE OF A SEARCH for a new pastor, conversations of various types will be held with candidates. Some conversations will take place with only one member of the committee: for example, to supply particular information, schedule a telephone interview or arrange a visit; other conversations will involve the whole search committee in a formal exchange of information and impressions. The search committee as a whole, and those members who have individual contacts with candidates, should be aware of the purposes of these conversations and prepare to handle them so that the greatest benefit to the search process comes from them. A record of all conversations should be made and stored in the candidates' files.

Types of Conversation and Information Gathered

The information that can be gathered from and imparted in conversations involving only one or two members of the search committee differs from that derived from a conversation involving the whole committee. The two types of conversation require different procedures.

Individual Conversations

The search committee may decide to limit conversations between candidates and individual members of the search committee. While individual contacts are necessary for such things as setting times for phone interviews, visits, and the like, these calls should be conducted in a businesslike manner. When a committee member calls to arrange a meeting, the candidate should be given a clear description of the proposed event (e.g., "We would like to schedule a speaker phone conversation with you and two or three search committee members" or "We would like to schedule a conversation with you followed by a meal together"). But the committee member should guard against developing a personal relationship with a particular candidate, which might be misleading to the candidate, create an unfair advantage later, or put the committee member in a compromised or awkward position.

Thus, contacts between individuals and candidates should be recorded. A notation of the purpose for the contact should be made, as well as any impressions the committee member had. Did the candidate seem to be organized and prepared to deal with a concern of the search committee (e.g., by having a calendar handy to schedule an event or being able to provide information that would be expected to be available)? In a case where a candidate contacts a member of the committee, was the question or reason for calling really necessary? A collection of impressions that are recorded can be valuable as the search proceeds.

Group Conversations

It is most important for search committees to prepare carefully for conversations with candidates in which the whole committee or a large part of it will be involved. These preparations include:

- Knowing what topics should not be discussed. According to federal law, there are some questions that cannot be asked of candidates. These include questions about age, physical characteristics, disabilities or chronic medical conditions, and national origin. Candidates should not be asked whether they have, or plan to have, children or what kind of childcare arrangements they make. In addition, the committee should not ask candidates if they have ever filed a lawsuit against an employer.

- Deciding on the purpose(s) of the conversation. For example, the initial conversation with a candidate should allow for an exchange of enough information that both candidate and committee can decide if they are interested in going deeper with one another. Later conversations can be more structured and focused in order to pursue points of mutual interest.

- Deciding what role members of the committee will play in the conversation. For example, many committees hold their initial conversations with candidates using a speakerphone. While the entire committee or a designated subgroup may listen to the conversation, it may be less stressful for the candidate if only two or three people actually participate in the questioning. Also, when the committee has prepared a list of questions for all conversations, it might decide that each question will be asked by the same individual for every conversation to create consistency in the interviews.

- Deciding how information gathered in the conversation will be recorded, discussed, and interpreted. When every member of the committee keeps notes on the conversation and shares what she has noted before a general discussion takes place, the participation of all (from the quietest to the most assertive) is ensured. The committee must decide how to develop and record the group's consensus about each conversation.

- Deciding how to ensure that preset guidelines are followed, e.g., on time limits (for individual participants and the whole conversation), or on encouraging the candidate to respond appropriately to questions, or on following up on candidate answers.

- Ensuring that an appropriate context of prayer is developed to frame and focus the conversation. A member of the committee might open the conversation, and the candidate might be asked to conclude it, with prayer.

Preparing for Conversations with Candidates

Clearly, the committee wants to learn as much as it can about candidates, but the candidates also want to learn as much as they can about the congregation in these conversations. The committee wants to discover how candidates' skills and characteristics compare with the congregation's criteria for a pastor. The candidates want to discern whether the congregation is a spiritual community where they can minister effectively. This kind of information is best exchanged in the form of a structured conversation. It is important to remember that committee and candidate can never discuss all the "what ifs" during the course of one conversation or even the whole search process; they want to get to know each other well enough to feel comfortable and confident in one another, and believe they can continue their spiritual journey together. A series of structured conversations offers an opportunity for getting to know one another better; each one should leave both candidate and committee eager to learn and reveal more.

The search committee should think about ways they can make the conversations as easy and comfortable for candidates as possible. Accordingly, after introductions (in a phone conversation, the people who talk should introduce themselves by name and say a few words about themselves— enough that the candidate can begin to associate voice and name), the committee might begin conversations with general questions such as: Would you tell us about your call to be a pastor? What do you like best about being a pastor? What things have you found difficult about being a pastor? If you had not entered the ordained ministry, what other vocation might you have chosen? Candidates for whom ministry is a later career might be asked: In what ways was your first career choice a natural lead-in to ministry or a contrast to it? Questions like these help establish a comfortable context for an exchange of information; they also help the committee to begin to learn if this is a person with whom they feel comfortable talking and whom they would like to know better.

Asking the Right Questions

As the conversation continues, the committee can move to areas of particular concern. Charles Ridley has refined methods to determine whether a candidate fits the ministry profile. As he has noted, past behavior is the best predictor of future behavior; questions should, therefore, be focused on what candidates have done in the past, rather than on what they would do in a hypothetical situation.[1] The committee should also avoid asking questions that will elicit opinions or yes-no answers. For example, the candidate might be asked to describe his spiritual discipline, or the ways he has helped parishioners grow spiritually. If the congregation has a large group of teenagers with whom a pastor will be expected to interact, the committee might ask the candidate if he has experience working with teenagers, but should follow up an affirmative answer by asking the candidate to tell about a teen program he has led or to describe a problem in a youth program that he discovered and the steps taken to address it. When the committee starts with a general question, they can ask follow-up questions based on a candidate's responses.

When candidates are either newly ordained or have become pastors after other careers, the committee can ask questions about things the candidates did in previous situations that relate to working in a congregation. All candidates can be asked to talk about their most important accomplishments and how they worked to achieve their goals. They can be asked to describe situations in which they have had to work to resolve conflicts or to revitalize or give a decent burial to an activity that was stagnant or failing. Likewise, they can be asked to talk about ways they convey a positive Christian witness, or how they have related to people who are unchurched.

Candidates' descriptions of their actual experiences can reveal not only information about the candidate's work in areas of interest to the congregation, but also a great deal about such important characteristics as whether the candidate can organize and tell a story, whether the candidate is personable, how the candidate exercises leadership, and whether the candidate consistently views life from a spiritual perspective.

Facilitating such a conversation requires preparation: the questions that are to stimulate the candidate's response must be as carefully prepared beforehand as were the exit conversation questions. Committee members should think about the kinds of answers they are likely to receive and decide whether or not that is the information they are looking for. The person(s) who will present the questions should be coached and rehearsed in their delivery. The committee might ask a neighboring pastor to conduct a practice interview with the committee and, at the end of it, offer some feedback on their process and their questions. The committee can then decide whether it is getting the kind of information it needs to evaluate candidates thoroughly, and revise its set of questions accordingly. As previously suggested, conversations can be structured so that core questions are asked of all candidates, but related questions or topics can be introduced when more discussion of a particular point is wanted.

The committee must decide ahead of time what they will do as the conversation develops. For example, what will they do if the candidate has not answered a question or has tried to redirect the conversation? Will the committee confront the candidate with a statement such as: "We don't believe you have answered the question we just asked," or simply note the diversion and go on? The committee should know how (and how many times) they will ask for clarification. They should decide how to follow up on a good response that makes them want to know more. The committee should also decide in advance if there is a maximum time they will allow for any conversation.

The Candidate's Questions

The committee should also allow time for the candidate to ask questions. These questions affirm the mutual discernment process

that is going on. They may also help the committee to determine whether the candidate has carefully read material such as the profile and to learn more about the candidate's interests and concerns. The committee should decide ahead of time how to choose a responder for each of the candidate's questions.

And, in Closing . . .

It is important for the search committee to remember that, just as candidates are revealing themselves in these conversations, so the search committee is revealing a great deal about the congregation to the candidates. A committee that affirms each candidate as a person with interesting and important things to say creates a much more favorable impression than one that projects an attitude of "Just the facts, Ma'am." Committees should strive to offer ways for candidates to expand upon bare facts and "tell their story." In this process, committee members may learn something about themselves as well as the candidates.

Conversations should always conclude with an explanation of how the committee will proceed from that point and information about when the candidate can expect to hear next from the search committee. And, of course, the candidate should be thanked for expressing interest in the congregation and for the time that has been shared with the search committee.

Note

1. Charles R. Ridley, *How to Select Church Planters: A Self-Study Manual for Recruiting, Screening, Interviewing, and Evaluating Qualified Church Planters* (Pasadena, Calif.: Charles F. Fuller Institute, 1989). A training program for the Ridley method of interviewing, "Training for Selection Interviewing," can be purchased as a kit from ChurchSmart Resources, Carol Stream, Illinois, (800) 253-4276.

WORKING TOWARD A FINAL LIST OF CANDIDATES

SEARCHES PROCEED DIFFERENTLY in various situations. In some contexts, the process allows little or no discretion for a congregation looking for a new pastor. For example, the middle judicatory executive may present the names of candidates in succession, one at a time, with the congregation's being required to reach a yes-no decision on one candidate before receiving the name of another. Or a short list of names from within the judicatory may be presented for a yes-no decision before the congregation is allowed to consider names from a wider area. While a congregation in such a situation cannot take all the steps outlined in this article, it should follow as many as possible (see PT 12).

This article looks specifically at searches in which congregations have greater freedom with regard to the number of candidates they may consider and the area from which they may consider them. Consider an extreme case: a search committee advertises widely for a position and receives over 100 expressions of interest, from all over the nation and even abroad. How does a search committee proceed to cut the list down to the most promising candidates? How does it get to know candidates, given the limitations of time, finances, and observing privacy rights?

The First Cuts

The search committee must find ways to get enough information about candidates to reduce the list to those who show the greatest promise for the congregation. In the extreme example, the search committee would go through the 100 or more initial applications and identify reasons why some applicants might be dropped immediately from consideration; for example:

- A pastor without congregation experience or whose experience is entirely in small congregations would probably lack the skills needed in a corporate-size congregation.
- A candidate's salary expectations might be beyond what the congregation could afford.
- A candidate may live somewhere so distant that visitations would be financially impossible.
- Several candidates may have described themselves in terms that do not come close to meeting the criteria the congregation profile and ministry description set out for the new pastor. On the basis of the initial information, the pool is reduced.

At this time (unless it has been done previously), the search committee may want to send remaining applicants a short list of questions to be answered in writing. These questions should elicit information about experiences the pastor has that are relevant to the search criteria. The answers to such questions allow the pool to be reduced further.

At this point, one candidate may appear to stand out from the rest and the committee might want to short-circuit the search process by singling that candidate out for early consideration. Under most circumstances, the committee should resist this temptation. First, a congregation might lose other good candidates if the "obvious" one does not work out. Also, if the "obvious" candidate goes through the process with others and still emerges as the final choice, the committee can have greater confidence that its decision was based on careful deliberation. Exceptions to this recommendation do occur rarely: if a congregation's needs are unique and a single candidate clearly meets those needs, the search committee might decide to confer with the judicatory (which is familiar with the congregation's situation), and discuss whether concentrating on this one candidate would be wise. In this case, the congregation should still follow the process described here for learning more about the candidate.

Phone Interviews

The most economical way of starting to learn about a candidate is through a phone interview (using a low-cost phone card). A member of the committee can call the candidate and agree upon a time for the conversation. The committee member should describe the format of the phone call (e.g., two or three members of the search committee would like to talk to you for 30 to 45 minutes, with other members of the committee in the room listening). These telephone conversations will reveal that certain candidates do not have the kind of experience the congregation needs and the inter-

action with other candidates may reveal unacceptable personal traits (e.g., failure to listen well, avoiding answering some questions, stiltedness). Final group evaluations of candidates (as outlined in the "Group Conversations" section of article PT 14) should allow the committee to narrow the field considerably. At this point, the committee may decide what is the maximum number of candidates it is practical or financially possible to pursue further, and continue on the basis of rankings by the whole committee. Occasionally, the decision not to visit certain candidates may disappoint one or more committee members who see something that appeals to them alone. In this case, the chaplain or process person can remind the committee of its commitment to working on the basis of agreement of a large (75 to 80 percent) majority.

Reference Checks

At this point, the committee must work toward developing a short list (e.g., no more than three) of candidates to bring for a visit to the congregation. The committee must aim to gather the greatest amount of information it can, within the expense limit budgeted for the search. To do this, the committee will want to visit and observe candidates in their home contexts to see how they conduct business and how they relate to people. At the same time, the committee will want to check references that the candidates have made available in their dossiers, identify other reference sources, and conduct document checks (see PT 16). Since these checks may take up to six weeks to prepare and also can entail sizeable costs, search committees need to decide early on at what point to initiate them, and how many they will initiate.

Despite the cost and effort involved, checking references is one of the most important aspects of gaining a deeper knowledge of candidates. First, consider the list of references a candidate provides. This will often contain names (typically about three) of people, lay and clergy, with whom a candidate has worked closely or studied, depending on age, position, and time out of seminary. The search committee must discuss what kind of information a particular reference may provide, and what kind of conversation would be most productive. For example, a church school superintendent would have a rather different perspective on a candidate than a seminary professor. The committee should designate a person to hold a conversation with each reference, and lay out in an informal way the kinds of topics to touch upon.

During the conversations with references, the search committee should try to take careful notes on the actual information the informant provides, but at the same time to be on the alert for clues to other matters. Is the reference person reluctant to discuss certain topics? Do replies to questions seem terse or guarded? How well does the reference person really know the candidate? The committee should schedule one or more meetings to listen to reports on conversations and discuss impressions that they leave. Did the conversations confirm material in the candidate's dossier, or did they suggest other areas to investigate?

The committee may also explore the possibility of finding and approaching additional sources of reference information. This is easier when a candidate lives and works relatively close by. But even in the case of distant candidates, it is often possible to recall that a former member of the congregation has moved to the candidate's area or that a close friend or relative of a committee member lives there. Original references can be asked to supply additional names. Information from such sources may be limited in depth and value, but any avenue that seems promising should be explored. A person calling such a reference can merely explain that Pastor X has expressed interest in the congregation's pastor position, and the search committee wonders if the reference knows the candidate and, if so, feels free to contribute any information.

The search committee must observe certain precautions in dealing with references. Some candidates may not want members of their home congregations (with a few exceptions) to know of their interest in a different position. In such a case, there should be a discussion with the candidate of how the committee might explore references without compromising the candidate's privacy. If the candidate is unwilling to allow the committee to approach enough suitable references, the committee must decide whether it can continue to consider that person.

A different kind of challenge arises in the case of a candidate who lacks congregation experience, either because she is just leaving seminary or, though ordained earlier, is in a noncongregational position (e.g., as a hospital or school chaplain, or in some nonclergy occupation). Candidates who have entered the ministry after working in a secular career for a period of time can present a similar challenge. In these cases, references from the former career cannot provide information about the candidate's functioning in a congregational setting, but can still provide valuable information if the committee has considered ahead what kind of relevant questions it can ask.

When information from these sources is gathered and analyzed, the search committee is in a better position to assess candidates and to decide whether to visit them in their home setting. This decision will be based on whether the visit appears to show enough promise for being productive and providing the kind of information the committee needs to justify the expenses involved. If the answer to this question is yes, the committee can make plans accordingly.

Visiting Candidates in Their Home Settings

The search committee must plan carefully for these visits. Consideration must be given to the time frame for the search, the geographical spread of candidates, the budget for the search, and the pool of committee members available for travel. It will be helpful if all visits can be made in the course of a month or so—this may suggest a top limit of about six candidates to be visited. Since the search committee will want to join in the major worship service(s) of the week (possibly sitting in groups of two), most visits will occur on weekends. An estimate of the total costs of all visits must be calculated to be sure that they fit within the funds budgeted for the search.

Forming Visiting Teams

Since a group of more than four could overwhelm a candidate or his congregation, the committee may decide to select different subgroups to visit various candidates; alternatively, one subgroup could make every visit if they have the confidence of the committee as a whole. If some committee members are already enthusiastic about a certain candidate, an uncommitted member on their team should balance them. Teams should also be balanced by gender and other factors (e.g., age, type of employment, theological views) as much as possible.

Visits must be scheduled with both candidates' and search committee teams' needs in view. Before any group goes out, the focus of visits must be determined and the committee must decide on a core of questions that will be asked. Teams should agree on how the visits will be conducted, arrange for recording of information obtained, and plan for the processing of information from the visits by the whole search committee.

A few words of caution at this point: the search committee should control its natural tendency to rush into these visits in a fit of exuberant optimism. The end of the search may appear to be in sight; people delight in travel to other locations with the responsibility to investigate; an element of competitiveness may develop among committee members as to who will go where and visit whom—some assignments will seem more attractive than others. The role of the chap-

lain or process person becomes critical at this point, focusing the committee on the need to continue with patient, prayerful care in following regular procedures. Now is not the time to spoil a search by haste and rashness.

Second, the committee must pay careful attention to the situations and needs of candidates. The visits will be impositions on candidates, intrusions in their lives that, though expected as a result of their candidacy, require those searching to exercise the greatest consideration in their dealings with candidates. If a search committee presents itself as overly demanding, it might suggest that the congregation will be a hard one to serve effectively as pastor. The sensitivity to candidates' situations that search committees display in arranging these visits will pay off in their effectiveness in both learning about the candidate and presenting the searching congregation favorably.

Planning for the Visits

The farther away a candidate lives, the more complex the travel arrangements will become. When dates have been agreed upon, a single person can make all travel arrangements; members of separate teams can also make their own arrangements. Of course, travel that involves airlines should be arranged well in advance in order to obtain the most favorable fares and schedules.

The committee must decide which factors each visiting committee will focus on before the visits begin by reviewing all the materials in each candidate's file and discussing any areas of particular interest. Each traveling group should plan the specific people it will speak to, and try to make arrangements for such meetings. The traveling group will also discuss how to arrange, in an unfamiliar place, to find out more about the candidate; for example, arrange contexts to observe or meet members of the congregation, look around the neighborhood for people outside the congregation to talk to, and observe the materials posted on bulletin boards, service leaflets, and other materials of interest. Each team might be asked by others to talk about their plans.

When a candidate is not serving in a congregation during the search, visiting teams will have to tailor their arrangements to the situation, learning as much as possible about how they work and interact with others in their special circumstances. At this point, there is something in every candidate's dossier that has made the committee want to know more. It is the visiting team's job to learn how these qualifications might be translated into the kind of role the search committee is trying to fill. Because the committee will want to see the candidate in the context of worship, a site where the candidate can serve as a worship leader must be found. It may be easiest for the candidate to arrange for such a site.

Processing Information from Candidates' Home Settings

The final task of visiting teams and search committee is that of preparing reports, listening to and commenting on them all, and deciding how to proceed thereafter. While each travel team will be familiar with the details of their visit and the conclusions they have reached, the entire committee will have to compare reports and decide which candidates will be brought to the congregation in preparation for the decision on a final candidate for the position (see PT 17).

The procedures described above may seem onerous—and they are, if carefully carried out—and the teams should therefore be prepared to undergo them in the right frame of mind. Periods of prayer, of free time for relaxation, and a spirit of friendly good humor and patience will go a long way to help the visiting teams and the whole search committee make a success of this project. The payoff for this success will be not only the discoveries that are made about candidates, but the favorable impression of the searching congregation that candidates—and all others with whom the visiting teams deal—receive.

MAKING BACKGROUND CHECKS

DURING THE DISCERNMENT PROCESS, congregations and judicatories can benefit from professional background checks on candidates. While it is possible for congregations to conduct these checks themselves, professional services may save time and provide more accurate results. Vital information that supplements the insights gained in conversation with the candidate's references can be obtained. Conducted with the permission of the candidate, these checks will provide reports on a candidate's credit and criminal history.

Because these checks can be expensive and may take up to six weeks, congregations and judicatories must determine the appropriate time to initiate the check. A congregation that has a small number of candidates may decide to begin the checks early in the process; a congregation with a larger number of candidates might wait until they have decided which candidates to visit in their home settings.

Services provided by document check suppliers include the following:

- Credit history: including name and address history, public records (tax liens, civil judgments, bankruptcy), credit card history, and history in loan payments, collections, and child support neglect.
- Criminal history: including felony and misdemeanor records, providing data on offenses, disposition dates, active warrants, dismissals, convictions, sentences, and conditions for each case. Searches of county-level jurisdictions, statewide jurisdictions, and federal district jurisdictions can be completed. Some restrictions may apply, depending on the jurisdiction. Fees can vary and a separate fee is applied for each jurisdiction searched.

Prior to initiating a search, it is advisable to consult with your legal counsel to develop policies and have approved a release form that candidates will sign to agree to the release of such information. Fair employment laws vary widely by state, and limits may exist on the availability of records.

Members of the search committee should be cautioned that all information derived from these document checks is strictly confidential.

Organizations frequently used to provide this information are:

Oxford Document Management Company
5701 Kentucky Ave N, Suite 115
Minneapolis MN 55428
(800) 801-9114
oxforddoc@aol.com

Professional Research Services
4901 W 77th St
Edina MN 55435
(952) 941-9040

Note

This article is drawn from material written by Richard M. Farrell. Used by permission.

PT 18

CANDIDATE VISITS TO THE CONGREGATION

WHEN A FEW FINALISTS HAVE BEEN IDENTIFIED, they are usually invited to visit the congregation. At this point, the search committee is very serious about getting to know the candidates and ready to incur the expense of bringing them and their spouse, if the candidate is married, to visit the community. Considering the number of separate events that will be scheduled for the candidate and the need to provide some private time for rest and reflection, the visit will usually be scheduled for a long weekend.

During this visit, the candidate will have an opportunity to meet with the search committee, board members, and members of the church staff and to observe the congregation at worship. The candidate should also be given the materials outlined in the section of preliminary steps found in PT 19. This visit provides an opportunity for the candidate to see the congregation in community and learn if he wants to be a part of it. Just as the congregation has been trying to discern whom to call as the next pastor, the candidates are discerning where they are called to continue their ministry.

A visit to a congregation places a candidate in unfamiliar surroundings. The candidate, who may previously have met only a few members of the search committee, will now be having conversations with the entire search committee. It is helpful if the candidate has the opportunity to meet with members of the board during this visit as well, particularly in situations where the board issues the call for a new pastor. Depending on denominational practices, the candidate may be asked to preach a sermon at the congregation or at a neutral site during this visit.

The candidate and spouse will be interested in seeing the larger community of which the congregation is a part; the search committee should ask if there are particular things they want to see as part of their visit before a final schedule is developed. For example, people with school-age children may want to visit local schools; a family with medical concerns may want to visit local doctors or hospitals; if the congregation does not provide church-owned housing, candidates may wish to tour the community with a realtor to see what their housing options might be. During this visit, the candidate may be expected to meet with a member of the judicatory staff. Some candidates may want to visit with other clergy of the same or other denominations in the community or region. Since the clergy spouse will not normally attend the candidate's conversations with search committee or board, it would be hospitable to offer the alternative of a planned activity or the opportunity for independent activities during those times.

Though many congregations are ready and eager to offer the candidate hospitality in the home of one or more members, candidates need their privacy and an opportunity for some downtime to relax, exercise, and pray and reflect on everything they have seen and heard. For this reason, it is preferable for the congregation to provide hotel accommodations for the candidate. While a member of the search committee will drive the candidate to scheduled events, a rental car would allow a candidate who has arrived by air to explore the community independently. Some mealtimes can be scheduled to offer the opportunity for a small group to meet and talk with the candidate; other meals can be scheduled with larger groups. Ideally, each member of the search committee should attend one small-group event with the candidate as well as one larger-group meeting.

Between Final Visit of Candidate(s) and Call

The candidate or candidates invited to the congregation have just left. No matter how many candidates have visited, the search committee has to agree on a recommendation to make to the governing board or congregation. Though candidates, board, and congregation might like a quick decision, the committee needs to weigh its decision carefully. How does it do this?

The committee should start with the recognition that no candidate is perfect; each one will have some characteristics that are just what the congregation is looking for and others that may work against the candidate's effectiveness in the congregation. The goal is to determine which candidates, if any, come close enough to matching the ministry description that was drawn up early in the search process. The committee should begin by reexamining the factual information that is known about each candidate (e.g., their experience, skills, interests, contractual expectations). The committee should also review the impressions about candidates that search committee members have formed during their contacts and conversations, as well as any feedback the committee has received from others who have met the candidates. The committee must weigh all this information and determine which candidate or candidates demonstrate a combination of personal qualities and experiences that allow them to be effective spiritual leaders in the congregation.

As information is reviewed, the committee should draw up a balance sheet for each candidate. Each committee member, in turn, should share their perceptions both pro and con; a scribe can record these observations, with no general discussion until every committee member has had the opportunity to participate. When all information is recorded, the committee should consider the points that have been raised and determine which ones represent a consensus about a candidate. Then plus and minus factors of the consensus must be weighed against each other; serious reservations about any candidate must be considered carefully, even if they are held by only one or two committee members. Such careful consideration will allow the committee to determine whether each candidate has the potential to be an effective pastor in this congregation, and can thus be recommended for a call.

The committee may find that it can recommend more than one candidate for a call; in this case, the committee should prioritize the candidates so that the board can offer a call in turn to other candidates if the first choice declines. If the committee decides, after prayerful consideration, that it cannot recommend any candidate, the search process must be extended or even started again. In this case, the search committee can express its willingness to conduct another search or ask to be replaced. Even if the search committee is willing to engage in another search, the board may decide to form a new committee.

In all of these situations, the chair

should be able to support the committee's recommendation, given the constraints that confidentiality continues to impose. The chair can list the principal findings on a candidate, comparing them with the ministry description and adding any additional factors that weighed in the committee's rec-ommendation. When the committee's recommendations can be supported with careful explanation, both search committee and board can feel confident that the recommendation for a call was made as the result of careful deliberation and consideration of all pertinent information.

PT 19

WORKING OUT A CONTRACT
WITH THE NEW PASTOR

THE SEARCH COMMITTEE has made its recommendation; the governing board or congregation has affirmed it. What happens now?

First, there is a joyous occasion: informing the selected candidate. This is usually the privilege of the board president. A phone call can be made after a board or congregation meeting that has voted on the selection. If the candidate has been told that a vote will be taken at a particular time and an unexpected delay occurs, the candidate must still be called and told that there has been an unexpected delay in reaching a decision.

What happens in this phone call? The caller expresses the congregation's happiness with the selection of this candidate and expresses the hope that the candidate will become their new pastor. The candidate may accept the offer at this point or ask for time in which to consider it. In the latter case, the caller will set a time at which to expect the candidate's answer. In either case, the caller asks if there is any more information of a general nature the congregation can provide. It is important for everyone to remember, though, that the public announcement of the call to the pastor should not be made until the formalities of the denomination (e.g., vote by congregation, signing of a letter of agreement) have been observed.

There is a natural tendency to assume the search process is complete when a candidate for pastor accepts the offer of a position. Search committee members, relieved that their task is completed, look only to return to a normal life. The transition committee may already be planning events to welcome the new pastor. The governing board, especially its president, looks forward to sharing responsibilities with the new pastor. But this is no time to lose focus. Much remains to be done to ensure that the new pastorate begins with clear understandings about the terms of the offer (e.g., salary, benefits, vacation, starting date) and who will work with the candidate to develop a contract or letter of agreement.

The contract or letter of agreement between pastor and congregation must be formulated and signed by the pastor and one or more persons in authority in the congregation. Sometimes the approval of the contract by the judicatory is required too. Some denominations and judicatories have standard basic forms that can be adapted to individual circumstances.

A copy of this document is given to every current board member and to new members as their terms begin. The board or pastor will refer to this contract when addressing any problems that may arise in their relationship. It is therefore extremely important that serious thought be given to this document; intense discussions between the new pastor and a representative of the congregation will have to take place. A good negotiation process and fair contract will do much to start the new pastorate in a positive atmosphere. Involvement of the judiciary may be required in the negotiations, or a transition companion can serve as advisor.

In these negotiations, assumptions that may have been held by both sides about the new pastorate need to be brought out into the open and differences in those assumptions addressed. The congregation may believe that their ministry description fully describes the pastor's responsibilities. The pastor may believe that things said by the search committee constitute a promise from the congregation. All statements about the nature of the position from the congregation and the pastor should be placed on the table, discussed, and formulated into an agreement the pastor and congregation can feel clear about and comfortable with.

The Negotiating Process: Preliminary Steps

It is not possible to set forth the matters that should be discussed in every situation, but the following suggestions can help lay the groundwork for a successful negotiation.

- The major expectations for the position should appear in the congregational profile or other materials that all candidates received. They should be discussed with candidates in the later interviews, when the search committee begins to find out more about the most serious candidates.
- Prior to the selection of final candidates, the governing board should see and approve in principle a letter of agreement or contract drafted by the search committee chair and board president. Some denominations have a boilerplate form for this agreement, with blanks where matters are nego-

tiable, such as compensation levels and benefits, which are tied to the position. The board should decide at this point if any terms are fixed and not subject to negotiation. Any nonnegotiable terms should be made clear to final candidates.

- Final candidates should receive copies of the judiciary's clergy personnel policies, if they exist. If the congregation also has a set of personnel policies for their clergy, they too should be provided.
- The congregation needs to have a clear statement of the terms of its health insurance policy (or that of the judiciary).
- The type of housing or housing allowance needs to be spelled out clearly. If a housing allowance is part of compensation, its tax consequences should be described. If the congregation provides housing, matters relating to responsibility for maintenance and upkeep (including, e.g., yard care and snow removal) need to be clear.
- During their visits to the congregation, finalists should have the opportunity to present any expectations they have for contractual matters.

The Negotiator: Mandate and Characteristics

The negotiator's mandate is to lay the foundation for a successful call, trying to reconcile the needs and characteristics of the selected candidate with the needs and resources of the congregation. The clergy person may negotiate for himself, or arrange for someone else to help represent his interests. The congregation's negotiator should be in close contact with judiciary staff to make sure that the agreement not only conforms with all applicable regulations and policies but also meets the standards of fairness and clarity that will promote an effective working relationship between pastor and congregation.

A good negotiator in these circumstances is someone who:

- has sound judgment and formal authority granted by the governing board;
- is prepared to work expeditiously at the candidate's convenience;
- wants the call to work, i.e., does not have significant reservations about the selected candidate;
- conveys a generosity of spirit, i.e., can represent the congregation's best interests while remaining sympathetic to the candidate's particular needs and situation. Generosity of spirit is especially important in dealing with financial matters, since clergy may not be comfortable or familiar with hard bargaining over money.

From Negotiations to Signed Contract

While the negotiations must proceed with care, there is need for rapid communication. Proposals for wording should be made in writing, and can be transmitted by e-mail or fax. If the negotiator feels the need to obtain the board's agreement to any point not already addressed, the board should quickly call a meeting to address the matter. If the judicatory's approval of the agreement is required or recommended, prior arrangements for securing this approval should be in place.

Although a well-drafted letter of agreement may be proposed and accepted without the need for further negotiation, it is still a good idea for the candidate to hear others' reactions to it, and for the candidate and congregation negotiator to go over the document point by point, discussing its ramifications. In the course of their discussion each party should become clearer about and more committed to the agreement.

Matters Covered in the Agreement

This outline addresses only the principal points to address in the agreement. It is not possible to recommend specific policies because of the wide variations within and across denominations and judicatories. Congregations, too, have traditional practices, and, of course, individual pastors have their own unique circumstances that may affect an agreement; for example, physical disabilities, military obligations, spiritual disciplines. The following issues are likely to arise in drawing up a letter of agreement.

FICA

Secular employers deduct FICA taxes (Social Security and Medicare) from regular employees' paychecks and the employer pays an equal amount. Clergy are considered self-employed, and thus are responsible for paying both employer and employee portions of the FICA. Many congregations pay clergy an additional salary supplement to represent what would normally be the employer's share of these taxes. This supplement becomes taxable income for the clergy. Arrangements for compensation of this type must be stated clearly.

Pension, Health, and Other Insurance

Congregation contributions to a clergy pension plan are generally expected, and rates are determined by the denomination. Health insurance is also generally provided to clergy through a plan offered by the judicatory or denomination. Most denominations or judicatories have a group life insurance plan that the congregation pays for. Disability insurance is becoming an increasingly popular option to protect both clergy and congregation, and in many cases this coverage is part of the denomination's pension and health benefit plan. In larger congregations, the benefit structure may be much more complex and tailored to individual needs.

Professional Expenses

A congregation reimburses its pastor for a range of expenses incurred in the normal performance of pastoral functions. These include travel, entertainment of parishioners or others in pastoral contexts, books and journals for professional use, and membership in professional organizations.

Often a denomination or judicatory will specify a dollar limit up to which expenses will be reimbursed, upon submission of documentation. Clergy and congregation should be clear about what kinds of expenses may be reimbursed, to what dollar limit, and what documentation will be required. Clergy may treat professional expenses beyond what a congregation reimburses as a federal and, in some cases, state income tax deduction. They are responsible for maintaining their own records of such expenses.

Housing

The value of housing provided by a congregation is considered income subject to what is generally called Social Security tax. It is not subject to federal income taxes, though it may be subject to income taxes in some states. This important benefit for clergy is also available for clergy who provide their own housing when part of the pastor's compensation is designated as "housing allowance." There must be a clear statement regarding any housing provision. For example, is $35,000 the stipend for a position, and an additional house or housing allowance will be provided, or does the $35,000 include the housing allowance? Normally, congregations that provide housing also pay for utilities and upkeep—but exactly what these terms include has to be made clear. Matters that should be spelled out include:

- Which utility bills does the church pay?
- How is maintenance provided for and decided on? Is there a budget for it?
- Under what circumstances may the congregation inspect the property to determine maintenance needs?
- Who cuts the grass, shovels the snow, and rakes the leaves?
- Who has authority to change the landscaping?

- Is it expected that there will be church activities in the house? Who decides this?
- Is the pastor expected to entertain the congregation or board in the house? Is there a budget for this?
- Will the house be painted or repaired before the new pastor moves in? When will this be done? How will decisions be made, e.g., about colors, wallpaper?
- What freedom does the pastor have to change things in the house?
- Are any structural changes needed at this time to accommodate a disability or special family need? When will this work be done?
- Under what circumstances might the pastor seek alternative housing? What approval is needed for this change?

Equity Allowance

Judicatories and denominations often mandate the compensation of clergy who are required to live in congregation-provided housing, because they will not have a chance to build up equity as they would if they owned a house. Each year, a congregation budgets a fixed amount or percentage of salary to be placed in an investment vehicle that becomes the property of the pastor. The equity allowance provides retiring clergy with a fund to invest in housing.

The Move and Start-Up Date

The agreement will state the date when the candidate assumes the position of pastor, and the date at which a salary increase or change in another benefit occurs. Some congregations try to move their pastor's changes in compensation matters to conform to their own budget year rather than counting from the day of the pastor's start of service. The negotiator will arrange the start of health and other insurance, pension payments, and salary payments, usually in coordination with the judicatory.

The contract should specify who will pay for the move, what the cost includes, and who will decide on the moving company. An approximate date for the move should be specified, especially if, for example, there is an agreement that the date of the move varies significantly from the start-up date. A pastor may want to delay a family's move until the end of school, for example, or to move into an empty house before the position officially starts. The congregation should be responsible for meeting the movers with payment and a key to the house.

Expectations Related to Pastoral Activity

The preceding matters relate to "nuts and bolts" issues of the pastor's contract. The agreement should also address important matters related to performance of pastoral activities.

Expectations on the Pastor's Time

It is hard to specify the working hours of a pastor. Some contracts specify the length of the clergy workweek in hours, days, or units such as a morning, afternoon, or evening. It may be easier to specify time off. Some agreements state that "the pastor is expected to preserve one continuous twenty-four-hour period per week solely for personal and family use." Another clause may specify that the pastor should have time off on national holidays, "taken in such a way as not to interfere with congregational worship or observances." Some congregations grant the pastor a Sunday off following Christmas and Easter. It may be desirable to specify the amount of time the pastor should be available in the church office.

Four weeks of annual vacation is standard. It should be specified how this time may be broken up into smaller units; for example, no more than four Sundays off for vacation purposes. Whether or not this vacation can be carried over from year to year should be specified. Two weeks of approved continuing education is also standard, but this should be described as "work-related training" and not as "leave."

In addition, the accrual of sabbatical leave at the rate of one month per year, which may not be used before the third or fifth year, is common.[1] The sabbatical leave is often scheduled to fit into a strategic planning process every four or five years. The middle judicatory probably has a policy on this. Because some church members invariably object to "all this time off," it is helpful to state in writing something like, "while in residence, the pastor is expected to be available at any time for genuine pastoral emergencies." In addition, the pastor should, whenever possible, publicize in advance periods of unavailability and should inform members of the congregation how to arrange for alternative sources of pastoral care.

Professional and Spiritual Development

Continuing education expenses and scheduling are handled differently in denominations, judicatories, and individual congregations. Usually a minimum dollar allowance and annual time allowance for continuing education are specified. How the money may be paid (e.g., can it build up over a period of years for a major project?) and when the time may be taken (e.g., not at major festivals, such as Easter) are matters for negotiation. Congregations may wish to go beyond minimums for their pastors, especially since benefits may accrue to them from this generosity.

Sickness and Disability

Few congregations specify or count the number of sick days a pastor takes, but an extended illness is a cause for real concern. Short-term disability insurance that takes effect after 30 days offers one answer; long-term disability insurance another. Oftentimes, a group of clergy in a congregation's area pull together to provide basic worship and pastoral services in an emergency (and during vacations). Retired clergy may also be a resource. The letter of agreement should attempt to address such situations.

Process and Schedule for Mutual Ministry Reviews

This is a critical element in the contract. Pastor and congregation should be clear when the pastor will be reviewed (and when the pastor will review the relationship with the congregation), who will do the reviewing, and the process that will be followed. Procedures to follow if serious differences arise should be set down. The consequences of these reviews, for compensation and conditions of service, should be discussed in the agreement (see PT 23).

Special Circumstances

The congregation and candidate may have unique concerns they wish the agreement to address. The pastor may have time commitments for military, national church body, or family responsibilities that should be recognized in the contract. A part-time pastor with another career outside the church should attempt to address possible conflicts that the dual role causes. Addressing such significant points in the agreement can avert misunderstandings in the future. The congregation may wish to include a more or less detailed "position description" which addresses specific things the congregation expects of the pastor and the terms of accountability, as an appendix to the contract. These details might be reviewed and revised by mutual agreement six months after the pastorate begins, and annually thereafter.

Changing or Terminating the Pastoral Relationship

The agreement should set out a procedure for amending the agreement by mutual consent; for example, as conditions of pastor or congregation change. It should also specify how the pastor may dissolve the relationship, for example, to move to a different position. The congregation may wish to set compensation if the pastor moves to another position without congregation approval before the first or second anniversary of the start of the pastorate. Dissolution of the relationship by the congregation is usually dealt with in denominational policies.

The agreement should also state what happens to the pastor's family if the pastor dies. How long will salary and benefits be provided? How long may they live in church-owned housing? The pastor will be relieved to know that the family will be cared for a certain length of time until it can readjust to the changed circumstances.

Conclusion

A well-drafted agreement will free pastor and lay leaders to work together without constant attention to details. By spelling out the conditions of the pastor's work, it will free the pastor for spiritual leadership in the congregation. The process of thinking about the relationship of pastor and congregation before the pastorate begins lays a solid foundation for the growth of the relationship.

Note

1. More information about pastor sabbaticals is available on videotape: Roy M. Oswald, *Why You Should Give Your Pastor a Sabbatical* (Bethesda, Md.: The Alban Institute, 2001).

WELCOMING THE NEW PASTOR

DURING A RECENT EXIT CONVERSATION with the departing pastor, the transition companion was shocked to discover that one of the pastor's issues was that he had never been formally installed. After 12 years in the congregation, it still bothered him. Further conversation revealed that the pastor and his wife were seldom, if ever, invited to visit the homes of members of the congregation for social events. During the exit conversation with the board, board members acknowledged this. Needless to say, the pastor was not leaving under the best of circumstances.

It is important that the congregation observe the formal rituals in welcoming the new pastor. In a very public way, they help establish the newly arrived clergy as part of and a leader in the community. Many judicatories have procedures for the formal installation of a new pastor. The board president should discuss, in an early conversation with the pastor, the congregation's desire for such an event, and offer to phone the judicatory to invite the executive or other representative from that office to officiate. The final date for such an event will be chosen with consideration for the schedules of everyone involved.

There are ways this event can mark this special time in the life of the congregation. The congregation should invite other pastors in the area, as well as community leaders. Having a reception or meal afterwards allows opportunities for those who attend to greet and welcome the new pastor (and pastor's family, if there is one). If possible, the service can be videotaped; this provides a permanent record of the service for both pastor and congregation, and allows homebound members the opportunity of seeing the service.

There are opportunities for a series of welcoming gestures for the pastor and family before the formal installation service. Someone can be designated to greet them the moment they arrive in town. If the pastor will be living in church-owned housing, it should be cleaned and ready for their arrival; flowers or a fruit basket would be a friendly greeting, as would a hot dinner for their first evening meal. While it is important not to overwhelm the new pastor and family with many drop-in visits in the first few days, a phone call checking to see that they have all they need to settle in would be appreciated. Soon after their arrival, someone can offer to provide a tour of the area and answer any questions that have arisen. In addition, someone from the congregation can let neighboring pastors in the same denomination know when the pastor is due to arrive, so they can offer a welcome as well. Neighboring pastors can also invite the new pastor to local prayer and study sessions, support groups, and other clergy activities. In many communities, the local newspaper will arrange to include an article that helps introduce the pastor to the community.

The congregation, in consultation with the pastor, may want to schedule a series of get-acquainted events (e.g., dinners, coffee hours, picnics). In addition, the pastor may want to schedule times for historical reflection (see PT 21) and identifying congregational norms (see PT 22).

When the new pastor has a family, the congregation should be prepared to welcome family members appropriately; however, care should be taken to avoid placing unrealistic expectations on the pastor's family members. Like any new members of the congregation, they will appreciate the opportunity to choose activities in which they want to participate.

When conducting research for *The Inviting Church,*[1] Roy Oswald and Speed Leas found that the way a congregation welcomes a new pastor is very similar to the way they welcome any visitor or new member. Thus, welcoming a new pastor offers an opportunity for the congregation to examine its hospitality practices and determine whether it needs to strengthen its ways of extending a welcome. As the new ministry begins, the congregation has the opportunity to grow in its relationships with old and new members.

Note

This article is based on material written by Richard M. Farrell. Used by permission.

1. Roy M. Oswald and Speed Leas, *The Inviting Church* (Washington, D.C.: The Alban Institute, 1987).

TELLING YOUR PASTOR
ABOUT THE CONGREGATION'S HISTORY

NO TWO CONGREGATIONS ARE ALIKE. Each has a unique mix of members and its own history. To become an effective spiritual leader, a new pastor has to take the congregation's people and history into consideration. Knowing about a congregation's past successes and failures helps the pastor know what kind of ministry is likely to be effective; knowing about the congregation's heroes and villains gives the pastor an idea about the types of people the congregation looks for and the kind it avoids; hearing about the leadership styles of the congregation's favorite former pastors shows the new pastor what kind of leader the congregation is looking for. Knowing about the congregation's past history can help the pastor identify areas where the congregation welcomes change, and areas in which tradition seems deeply entrenched.

An occasion set aside for historical reflection can provide the new pastor with much of this information, as well as help the congregation to reflect upon their past and look toward the future with their new leader. Following a meal, the congregation spends time recalling all the important things that happened in previous pastorates. To be most productive, it is important to collect and preserve the recollections in an orderly fashion. Some suggestions for doing this include:

- Choose a facilitator who can encourage sharing of ideas without allowing the process to get bogged down. Someone uninvolved in the congregation's history who can be impartial (e.g., a neighboring pastor or lay leader) may be the best choice. A skilled leader from within the congregation must make a conscious effort not to influence the history that emerges with her own recollections or bias about them.

- Choose a couple of scribes to record information as it emerges. Having two scribes will allow them to record comments quickly. The newest members of the congregation may be a good choice: they will have the least to say and come with fewer prejudgments, but still would enjoy being involved in the event.

- If space permits, record information on a single long sheet of newsprint, beginning at the right end with the most recent pastorate (a timeline will emerge as comments about earlier pastorates are recorded to the left). If posting space is limited, newsprint tablets can be used, with completed sheets about each pastor posted at different locations and kept in chronological order.

- Begin with recollections of the most recent pastorate, that is, the one that al-

Sample Recollections of Recent Pastorates

Pastor Paul Schwartz (1983–1991)	Pastor Peter Buhler (1992–1995)	Pastor Joanne Abel (1995–2003)
• Hired our first youth worker. • Changed the Sunday morning schedule. • Our steeple collapsed in a storm.	• Started a boy scout troop. • Formed a men's group. • Youth group traveled to Taizé. • Neighbors complained about church parking.	• Renovated the sanctuary. • Started handbell choir. • Held confirmation retreats. • Church building was broken into. • Emphasis on tithing.

most everyone will recall and probably the one about which most information will be shared. The facilitator will encourage people to recall significant things that happened in the congregation's life. When people seem to have recalled the important events for one pastor, the group should focus on the pastorate immediately before it, and so on. An hour or so should be allowed for this entire process.

As the evening continues, the recollections may look similar to the table above. There will, of course, be much more under each of these pastorates. Some will contain several columns of material.

After this work is completed, the facilitator divides people into groups of six or eight and gives each group a single sheet of newsprint. Each group is asked to reflect on the question, "What can we say about our congregation based on this review of our history?" and write down their five most significant generalizations. Some groups have found that newcomers are most able to articulate these generalizations because they have less personal involvement in the events. After about 20 minutes, the groups come together. Each group presents and posts its written summary to lead up to the final activity of the evening. As each new list is presented, duplicate statements can be removed by group consensus so that any statement appears only once.

The last stage of the process is quick: each person in the room is given three brightly colored dots and asked to place them on the three generalizations that he feels are the ones the new pastor should consider most important. The generalizations receiving the most dots represent the congregation's areas of greatest concern.

If congregation leaders do not offer to hold such an event, the new pastor should request one, saying, "I really want to know who you are as a congregation. I have a guide for facilitating an event to reflect about the congregation's history, and I'd like to figure out how we could conduct it."

Historical reflection is usually fun for everyone. Many congregations enjoy leaving the newsprint up on a wall for several weeks after the event, so that those who could not attend can still recall or learn about the congregation's history. Long-time members enjoy talking about their history; newcomers learn a lot and gain an appreciation for the congregation they have just joined. The new pastor gains a sense of the congregation's history, and a good sense of the congregation's perceptions about itself. In addition, the pastor has the advantage of hearing the high points of the congregation's history at one time, with many points of view on various points represented. Talking about the congregation's history together allows pastor and congregation to discover some of the most important areas for their work together.

PT 22

DISCOVERING THE CONGREGATION'S NORMS

EVERY HUMAN COMMUNITY has norms (un-written, unspoken, and often unconscious rules about the "way things should be done") that govern the behavior of its members. In congregations, norms may develop as a result of an event, such as when children playing in the kitchen started a fire 20 years ago, and children still are not allowed to enter the kitchen without an adult. Or, norms may also develop because of habit; for example, people are never considered for election to the board until they have attended the church for at least three years. While members of the congregation may not think about their norms, newcomers may become aware of them quickly. Newcomers who are comfortable with the norms will fit into the congregation easily; those who are uncomfortable with them will probably go to another congregation where things feel right. It is a little different for a pastor: as a newcomer, the pastor may see a norm that is hindering ministry some way and try single-handedly to change it. Almost certainly, trouble will follow, unless there is a large consensus from those present that this should be changed.

The beginning of a new pastorate offers an opportunity for a congregation to discover and examine its unwritten practices as part of the process of introducing the congregation to the new pastor. A con-gregation that decides to bring to light and examine the hidden understandings about how it goes about its business will be better able to start the pastorate on the right foot and make any adjustments that seem appropriate. This process can have several benefits. The new pastor will be less likely to make mistakes because of inexperience or inaccurate assumptions. Relatively new members can learn about expectations and test them against their own experiences. (If the congregation has thought of itself as welcoming, have newcomers in fact been welcomed?) Committees may have become self-perpetuating, not adjusting their focus to reflect the congregation's evolving mission. (Should outreach activities be devoted to international concerns in the light of growing needs in the local community?) A process that brings to light and discusses the traditions is a high priority.

An Event for Examining Unwritten Practices and Expectations

A good way to conduct this process is to devote time to examining how the congregation behaves and what its expectations are. Such an event will resemble the one of historical reflection, although its focus will be quite different. The first requirement is to recruit a leader. An outsider—the pastor of

66

another congregation, a transition companion, or an experienced lay volunteer from another congregation—may be the best choice for facilitator, because that person will probably have a less biased perspective. The facilitator should meet ahead of time with the new pastor and a small group from the congregation to determine areas where the pastor and leaders suspect current norms are inhibiting ministry, or about which they think discussion is needed.

These areas might include:

- *Worship.* What kinds of lay participation do we want in worship? What kind of music do we prefer? What kind of sermons do we want?

- *Male and female roles.* What are the expectations of men and women? What roles or activities have traditionally been reserved for either men or women?

- *Children.* How are they expected to behave in different contexts? Are preschoolers excluded from certain things?

- *Use of the church buildings.* What sorts of things do we expect to happen outside of church services? What do we expect of members and community groups that use the building? How is the use of the buildings monitored?

- *Money matters.* Who knows how much various people give to the church? In what circumstances are money matters an acceptable topic of discussion? What do we do when we have a shortfall? What would we do with a large bequest?

- *Welcoming people.* How do we welcome or not welcome people? Do we welcome different groups of people in different ways? Are there any people we would not welcome?

- *Conflict.* How do people express disagreement with one another? Are people welcome to express an opinion that differs from the majority? When peo-

ple disagree, do they deal with it at the time, or argue later in private? Is gossip tolerated?

- *Membership.* What does membership in the congregation entail? Are there different categories of members? Are they recognized in appropriate ways? When is someone considered a member of the congregation?

The event begins with a group session in which the leader talks generally about the nature of unwritten practices and expectations. The leader can then introduce one of the topics that have been identified (written at the top of sheet of newsprint), and lead the group in discussion of the topic, writing down the group's thoughts about the congregation's unwritten rules. When discussion of this topic is completed and people understand how to examine the topics, the leader can introduce the other topics (also on newsprint), posting the sheets of paper at different locations in the room.

The leader can then ask that those interested in each topic go stand by the sheet. If more than half a dozen people are standing by a topic sheet, the facilitator can either divide the group into smaller groups that would all address the topic, or ask whether anyone would be willing to join another, smaller group. After the group sizes have been adjusted, the small groups take their sheet down and go to a table where they can work comfortably. (If several groups will address a topic, extra groups can take a blank sheet of newsprint and write the topic on the top and then proceed as instructed. If overall participation is small, some groups may have to discuss two related topics.) Each group should appoint a scribe, and spend about 30 minutes developing its list of practices and expectations related to the topic.

After the small-group phase, the whole group reassembles and the leader asks each group to present its list of practices and expectations. There is no discussion beyond clarification. After all the data have been presented, however, the leader asks people which observations match their experience, strike them as "most true," or are personally most important to them. People who disagree can also be asked to note and explain their opinion. This phase should take 30 to 45 minutes.

The critical point of the exercise is reached in a final discussion in which the leader asks people which norms they would like to change. People may notice things that make them uncomfortable—practices that, when brought to consciousness, are different from what people actually want. A short list of up to six points should be developed.

This list may both enlighten and challenge the congregation. Some points may call for action, but that is not the work of this session. Those in leadership roles in the congregation will have to decide how to take appropriate steps to deal with the discoveries of the meeting. If the discussion has uncovered an unhealthy congregational practice (e.g., a tendency to gossip about people with whom one disagrees), the leadership team may decide to develop a behavioral covenant that could be adopted and en-forced in the congregation. Ongoing communication with the congregation will be necessary, and working together to solve a problem can reinvigorate people.

A time spent identifying and examining congregational practices and expectations, as well as a time for historical reflection, are two gifts a congregation can give its new pastor. Yet these two activities can result in much more than simply providing the new pastor with information about the congregation. Both activities hold real potential for congregations to examine themselves and identify certain things they would like to do in a more positive manner. In addition, there is the potential for real bonding to take place during these events, not only between pastor and congregants, but also among congregants themselves. This is a natural byproduct of having people come together to explore where they have been (history) and how they have behaved along the way (practices and expectations). Both experiences provide members the opportunity to share their perspectives about the congregation, help the new pastor to minister more effectively to the congregation, and offer ways for the congregation to support the new ministry.

PT 23

EVALUATING THE MINISTRY
OF PASTOR AND CONGREGATION

THE CONGREGATION'S PROFILE and ministry description used in the search phase provide information about the kind of pastor a congregation is looking for and the kind of relationship it hopes to develop with the pastor. The letter of agreement or contract with the new pastor attempts to give these expectations and hopes a clearer form. But it is impossible to prescribe exactly what will happen in a congregation when a pastor takes up a new call. Relationships among people develop in unpredictable ways, and congregations, like all human institutions, are in constant flux. How can a congregation, at the beginning of a new ministry, take steps to foster positive developments in the pastor-congregation relationship and in the new pastor's ministry? A successful beginning produces the seeds of continued adaptation over the years that follow.

Mutual Ministry Review

The start of a new ministry is nurtured by monitoring the pastor-congregation relationship. A congregation should want to learn about how the pastor is doing in the start-up phase of the ministry and how the congregation is responding. The term *mutual ministry review* is commonly used to describe this process. The congregation and pastor examine together what the pastor is

doing and how the pastor does it, as well as what the congregation is doing and how they are responding to and supporting the pastor. In this way, pastor and congregation can begin to identify and develop the strong points of their life together, as well as addressing things that might work against the development of a productive relationship.

It may at first appear that the congregation is reviewing the pastor and the pastor the congregation, but in this process pastor and congregation each get to look at themselves, too. The reviews become mutual experiences in which both pastor and congregation expose themselves to the hazards of self-discovery. The beginning of a pastorate is the time to face the facts that human beings are imperfect, that relationships undergo change as outside conditions have an effect on them. However, people of good will, working intentionally, can overcome some of their imperfections and, by addressing shortcomings of their performance, improve themselves and their relationship with one another. Essentially, the ongoing review of pastor and congregation by one another entails the establishment of a means of communication with one another in an atmosphere of evolving trust and concern.

A pastor and congregation that communicate effectively will both come to realize that there is more to the other than they realized during the search process. Each has to adjust initial assumptions in the light of both positive discoveries (e.g., the pastor's discovery that many in the congregation are happy to volunteer for worthwhile tasks) and negative ones (e.g., the congregation's discovery that the pastor does not like to ask people to perform trivial but necessary tasks more than once, and as a result some things may not get done). The opportunity to mention such things in a safe context before misunderstandings arise facilitates the addressing of more significant differences that may arise later. Another article in this handbook (see CT 6) discusses the "honeymoon period" of a new pastorate, when neither pastor nor congregation is willing to voice any criticism of the other. That article shows the need for vehicles in which comments about the developing relationship can be made.

One excellent model is to hold quarterly mutual review sessions involving the pastor and the board or a smaller committee with this function. A good way to elicit remarks that bring underlying issues into the open at these sessions is to pose some simple questions as the focus for silent reflection and then response by all present. Such questions might include the following:

1. What would you like more of from me? (What do you want me to start doing?)
2. What would you like less of from me? (What do you want me to stop doing?)
3. What would you like me to keep the same? (What do you want me to keep doing?)

Both pastor and congregation members present will assume that they are being asked these questions by the other and will address them accordingly. In the period of reflection (five to ten minutes, or more if needed), all should note on paper the points that they will expand on in the exchange of answers that follow. The process will probably work best if the pastor addresses the questions aloud first. A pastor's candor and sincere attempt to grapple with the issues can encourage members to address issues with similar honesty and openness. Those individual members then give their responses. No discussion (except for clarification of what was said) takes place during this phase of the mutual review discussion.

When this information is out in the open, discussion can take place. Members may have said they had hoped the new pastor would visit members in their homes. The pastor might explain that unexpected duties had preempted some home visit time, and some members had made such visits difficult to arrange. The pastor might note that the congregation has said that Christian education is important, but that she has had little success finding teachers. The committee might explain that many people feel they lack the skills to teach effectively. After all perspectives on each issue have been heard, pastor and congregation members need to discuss how each concern can be addressed. The pastor might ask the committee to help prioritize the concerns, so that the most important ones can be addressed first. The pastor may also ask for lay involvement or leadership in some activities to help them be more effective. Working together, pastor and committee can determine which things should be done by the pastor, which things could be done by members, and which will work best with the involvement of both. The plan of action and expectations for themselves and each other can be stated, and then can be subjects of discussion at the next review session.

Assuming that the quarterly review sessions of the first year of a new pastorate go well, the pastor and board can move to less frequent sessions. It is a good idea to conduct a comprehensive review of the relationship between pastor and congregation after four or five years, in order to ensure that some issues, deeply embedded in the congregation's life, have not escaped notice. (A productive format for this occasional mutual ministry review is the study of Revelation 1–3, which is described in the article about developing the congregation profile; see PT 9.) This comprehensive review of the congregation's ministry should be a prelude to the development of a new strategic vision for the congregation. Why not take all that has been learned in such a comprehensive review and plan to do something about it? The pastor's sabbatical should follow immediately after such a new strategic vision is formulated. He will need rest and additional training to move the congregation forward. Between comprehensive ministry reviews, there should be at least one annual reflective period between pastor and governing board to explore if the ministry is still on the right track.

Pastor-Initiated Evaluation

There may be times when the pastor decides to initiate a process of "personal growth evaluation" to examine certain aspects of the pastor's own ministry, and facilitate personal development. This process is different because the pastor is in control (deciding what aspect of ministry will be examined) and owns the data. If, for example, the pastor senses that the congregation is not responding well to her sermons, she may ask a couple of trusted lay leaders (who can maintain absolute confidentiality) to interview half a dozen people after one sermon a month. They are to find out what people like and dislike about the sermons, and if they have other concerns relating to sermons. After the data have been gathered, the pastor meets with the lay leaders, hears what they have to report, and discusses the significance of their findings with

them. If the pastor sees concerns that can be addressed (e.g., people feel sermons are too political, too "scholarly," too predictable) she can attempt to remedy the situation. The pastor may decide not to make major changes, but to preach a sermon about the process and purpose of preaching, and then ask for wider congregational feedback.

Or the pastor could ask a couple of lay leaders to help devise a questionnaire on a particular set of issues to administer to some subset of the congregation. These lay leaders could then help the pastor interpret the results. The outcomes from such measures are controlled entirely by the pastor, however. If board members ask what the pastor has learned from the questionnaire, the pastor might say, "I initiated this process for my own learning and personal growth. At some time, I may be ready to talk about what I've learned, but I'm still working on it." What will be shared and when it will be shared is entirely the pastor's decision. This kind of process requires that the pastor take the lead in finding out what impact she is having on members, and that a built-in safety mechanism allows the exploration of potentially sensitive issues before they reach crisis level.

This discussion has moved beyond the beginning of a pastorate, but it emphasizes the point that the congregation and pastor can and should work together to create an atmosphere of openness and acceptance. A pastor and congregation that encourage and foster this atmosphere are already on their way to beginning ministry together.

PART 2

ENRICHING TRANSITION

Making the Most of the Interim Period

Congregations often think of an interim period as something to get through as quickly as possible. They think that rapidly finding and installing a new pastor will ensure stability and "allow things to return to normal." But a slower and more introspective transition period will allow the congregation to understand itself, recognize and address problems that are standing in the way of congregational health, identify areas of growth for the future, and through this process understand the characteristics that it should eventually look for in a pastor. In short, a longer transition will allow opportunities for congregational renewal.

Any congregation will have to make adjustments when a pastor leaves. William Bridges, formerly on the faculty of Mills College and now a business consultant who has written books and led seminars on the relationship between change and transition, notes, "It isn't the changes that do you in, it's the transitions. *Change* is situational: the new site, the new boss, the new team roles, the new policy. *Transition* is the psychological process people go through to come to terms with the new situation. Change is external, transition is internal."[1] Bridges goes on to argue that if people in an organization do not go through a transition of their own to adapt to a change, the change will be destructive rather than constructive. Many great ideas fail because people in organizations resist the reality of change and the new patterns of doing things that follow.

Bridges claims that we must expect challenges as a natural part of the transition process. If we do not we are likely to try to rush through it and become discouraged when we cannot make the transition. Though this can be a painful time, a transition is an individual's and an organization's best chance for creativity, renewal, and development.

The Developmental Tasks

In the mid-1970s, Loren Mead first articulated five "developmental tasks" of a congregation in search of a pastor.[2] They are:

1. Come to terms with your history.
2. Become clear about your identity.
3. Allow shifts in leadership to occur.
4. Rethink the linkages to your denomination and its structures.
5. Make a commitment to new leadership and a new future.

Come to Terms with Your History

William Bud Phillips, former director of the Centre for Study for Church and Ministry and now dean of the Vancouver School of Theology, suggests that this step involves identifying both personal and organizational losses.[3] Congregations that do not acknowledge the loss they feel with the departure of the pastor will have trouble bonding with the new pastor. Further, the congregation should examine its past and identify the highs and lows that have occurred through the years.

Coming to terms with history entails an open exploration of the total history of the congregation and learning from watershed events, both highs and lows. Done well, it helps members understand and accept who they are and how they got there so they can move into the future. It is a process of "letting go," enhancing the process of grieving, helping people to enter into their pain in order to look forward in hope.

Become Clear about Your Identity

A self-study makes a substantial contribution to this task if the process is open to the congregation as a whole (see PT 9). Often, congregational leaders focus on producing a document for finding the next pastor and so miss a key opportunity to discover and include the wider perspectives of members in the self-study. The process is more important than the product here. When members of the congregation are not involved in the process of self-study they lose a sense of ownership in the ensuing statement of "who we are." Persons left out of the process are less likely to be committed to new leadership (i.e., the next pastor) if they feel that their own wants, needs, and goals have not been reflected in the congregation's statement of its goals.

The interim period provides a good opportunity to determine whether a congregation's perception of itself is accurate. The self-study will reveal the makeup of the congregation's membership and allow for examination of existing programs and a determination of whether they are meeting members' needs. For example, does the education program of the congregation meet the needs of members of all ages? Does the

study reveal that there are many families with small children or does the church have an increasing population of older members with unmet needs? The self-study can describe how the congregation fits in to the surrounding community and identify the congregation's sense of mission. For example, if the population of the community surrounding the church has changed significantly with regard to ethnicity, income, or age, the congregation may realize that its programs are not responsive to the needs of people in its neighborhood. Being clear about its identity will help a congregation to address some of the most challenging issues that seem to hold them back from being all that they could be.

Allow Shifts in Leadership to Occur

Lay leaders in a transition are often those who worked best with the previous pastor. Now the roles of clergy and laity are undergoing change. Some lay leaders are ready for a change, some may be burned out, while others want to shape the church's future by remaining in positions of power, either to promote or to resist change. The interim period is a time to review leadership selection and decision-making processes, empower all individuals and groups in the congregation, educate members on the existing leadership structures, and explore changes in those structures that will enhance the health of the congregation (see ET 3).

Rethink the Linkages to Your Denomination and Its Structures

During the interim period, the importance and place of denominational systems in the life of any congregation are as much in transition as is the understanding of leadership roles. Congregations connect to their denominational systems on the basis of both formal structures and the relationship of the pastor with the key people in their denominational offices. If the previous pastor has provided little connection, the interim period offers the opportunity to create links.

One of the realities that mainline denominations face is the movement of members across denominational lines. Members of a congregation who come from other traditions may not understand why their new church does things a certain way. The interim time offers an opportunity to educate members on denominational policies and practices. The services that judicatories offer to congregations in a transition can forge a renewed sense of linkage.

Make a Commitment to New Leadership and a New Future

Loren Mead wrote, "It is one thing to hire a new pastor. It is quite another thing for a congregation to enter a commitment to a new ordained leader and to the possibility of new tasks and missions. The difference between those two sentences is the difference between a parish that does not do this fifth developmental task and one that does it."[4] There is a real distinction between a congregation that wants its new pastor to keep things going just as they were, and a congregation that sees each pastorate as a time for them to move to a deeper and possibly different relationship to God and their way of serving God. Unless a congregation can commit to new leadership and a new future, complaints and resistance are likely to hinder the relationship with the new pastor.

If a congregation decides to use the transition time intentionally, it can proceed on its own, or may find the services of an intentional interim pastor helpful. In either case, the Interim Ministry Network resource edited by Roger Nicholson, cited in PT 7, would be helpful.

It will take time and effort to accomplish the five developmental steps outlined above; however, the benefits reaped by the congregation that does accomplish them can be significant. R. Neil Chafin, an experienced consultant who helped start the Center for Congregational Health associated with the Southern Baptist Hospital in Winston-Salem, North Carolina, puts it this way: "The way a congregation chooses to use its interim time will shape congregational growth, identity, and health for years to come. We also know that what is done in the interim time really determines whether the new minister and congregation will form a solid ministry team."[5] It is important, therefore, that a congregation that cares about its future take time to think through carefully how it should deal with the interim period.

Notes

1. William Bridges, *Managing Transitions: Making the Most of Change* (Cambridge, Mass.: Perseus Books, 1991), p. 1.

2. Loren Mead, *The Developmental Tasks of the Congregation in Search of a Pastor* (Washington, D.C.: The Alban Institute, 1977).

3. William Bud Phillips, *Pastoral Transitions: From Endings to New Beginnings* (Washington, D.C.: The Alban Institute, 1988), ch. 5.

4. Mead, *Developmental Tasks*, p. 7.

5. Excerpted from Intentional Interim Ministry, an undated and unpublished paper developed by the Center for Congregational Health in the early 1990s.

ET 2

THE ROLE OF TRANSITION COMPANION

THE BEGINNING MINISTRY TOGETHER PROJECT was started in the 1990s by people from two middle judicatories who were concerned at the number of poorly managed pastoral transitions they had seen. The damage to congregations from such transitions motivated them to find ways to anticipate and counter tendencies to error on the part of their congregations. These judicatories faced an increase in the number of difficult pastoral transitions, along with a pinch in financial resources that kept them from expanding their staffs to address the need for enhanced support services. The use of trained volunteer paraprofessionals to perform services to complement the things that only professional judicatory staff could do was one answer; this book was another.

In the early stages of the project these paraprofessionals were thought of as resembling consultants, but since that term suggested professional preparation, the term *companion* was adopted. It reinforces the basic role of the position—that of offering advice as it shares with a congregation the many stages of a pastoral transition.

The Nature and Functions of the Transition Companion

In order to fulfill the role of companion to a congregation throughout a pastoral transi-tion, the transition companion must have experience with and training in such transitions. Experience by itself does not necessarily provide the perspective on the whole process and the possible variety of situations. A transition companion is trained to help a congregation in transition especially by:

- advising pastor and congregation on appropriate ways to close out the ministry that is ending;
- holding an exit interview with the departing pastor (or governing board or both);
- helping to form and organize a transition committee;
- advising on the formation of a search committee;
- recommending ways to prepare a congregation profile and ministry description of the next pastor;
- attending meetings of the search committee to help it observe correct procedures and maintain a focus on the spiritual dimension of its task;
- advising the board on its dealings with an interim pastor (if there is one); for example, on a contract, review of the interim's work, an exit interview with the interim;
- coaching the search committee on interview techniques and arrangements;

- advising on a letter of agreement with a new pastor;
- recommending to the transition committee ways to welcome the new pastor and family to the congregation and community;
- discussing with the new pastor how best to become familiar with the congregation;
- helping the board and new pastor develop a review process and pastor/parish relations committee;
- advising the congregation on closing out the transition process, recognizing those who served on the transition and search committees and in other ways.

This list suggests both the range of things a congregation needs to be aware of in a transition and the desirability of having on hand throughout a resource to turn to when questions arise. To be sure, congregations can manage a transition themselves, especially with guides such as an interim pastor and this book. But the presence of a companion adds an important dimension: the human one. A transition companion can give an instant answer to a question and eliminate the need to look one up. More than that, a companion can foresee that certain steps might be unwise or counterproductive, sense when differences on a committee are growing into personal conflict, and recall people to their spiritual responsibilities when they are in danger of being overlooked.

A companion, then, is not just an adviser but a friend, the kind who can stop or prevent you from doing something rash and against your own interests, and who can also help a congregation and its leaders to discover the best in themselves.

Selection and Training of Transition Companions

Since the transition companion will perform services that a judicatory could provide if it had the personnel, the selection, training, and deployment of companions

are usually concerns of a middle judicatory. The involvement of judicatory staff members in a number of pastoral transitions will help them identify lay and ordained people who seem fitted for this role. They can look for people who have the general skills, experiences, and qualities that a companion needs to have. These include:

- practical experience in one or more transitions;
- common sense and good judgment about the behavior of groups;
- ability to maintain absolute confidentiality;
- ability to command the respect and trust of a wide range of people;
- firm spirituality and devotion to their own congregation;
- the courage to speak and act in accordance with firm principles;
- a respect for fairness and observance of proper process.

Normally a judicatory will arrange for training specific to the denomination and judicatory. The Beginning Ministry Together project has offered training sessions, and some judicatories have developed their own forms of training, either alone or in cooperation with others. A number of individuals, clergy and lay, have received specialized training to offer these training sessions.

When suitable persons have been identified and have agreed to explore the role and function of a transition companion, a training session is arranged. Afterwards, those willing to serve as companions are added to the list of companions their judicatory maintains and, as soon as possible, are made available to congregations in transition. The transition companions in some judicatories continue their training informally by holding joint meetings to discuss and comment on their experiences.

Arranging for Transition Companions

When a judicatory learns that the pastor of one of its congregations will leave or retire, it takes steps to advise and assist the congregation's governing board on its procedures and expectations for the process. The congregation may be offered or assigned the services of a transition companion as part of the introduction to the transition process. If the congregation has to make a choice about whether to use a companion, it should consider these factors:

- *Transition experience.* If the pastorate now ending has been a long one, few or no members may have experience with a transition. Considering the rapidity of change in procedures and clergy culture, recent experience is highly desirable.

- *Objectivity.* It is much easier for someone from outside the congregation to keep a more detached attitude to the process, ask tough questions, and offer candid feedback.

- *Prayerfulness.* It is easy for members of a search committee to be distracted by the details of the search process and fail to rely on the work of the Spirit. A companion knows how and when to intervene to keep a group grounded in prayer.

- *Focus.* A companion has the skills to help a group concentrate on its task and avoid unproductive diversions. Congregation members may be unwilling to take on this function themselves.

- *Encouragement.* In a long and arduous search process, a companion can reassure the search committee about the need for patience and commitment to the process. The companion can refer to similar searches that, though long, turned out successfully.

- *Facilitation in communication.* The companion, with a knowledge of the interim pastor (if any), the judicatory, and the congregation, can advise on the appropriate roles of each and how to communicate among them effectively.

- *Perspective.* Although members of the congregation will fill the significant roles during the transition, a companion will have a clear view of the entire process and can help provide continuity from beginning to end.

Arrangements between Congregation and Transition Companion

When a congregation has decided to accept or has been assigned a companion, arrangements must be made and agreed to by both. The congregation needs to understand what the companion can and will do and what its responsibilities are to the companion. The agreement should result from a conversation in most situations; it can take the form of a simple letter that summarizes the understanding they have reached. The discussion should reach agreements on such points as the following.

- *Time commitment.* Will the companion be expected or merely encouraged to attend all meetings of the search committee? The transition committee? The governing board?

- *Compensation.* Will the companion's travel expenses be reimbursed? If so, on what basis? Will the companion receive other compensation?[1]

- *Roles and responsibilities.* Will the companion serve strictly as an advisor or will he be expected to assume a more active role (e.g., as facilitator) on occasion? To serve as chaplain? To provide written reports to the search committee or board?

- *Contact person(s) for the companion.* The companion's contract with the congregation should specify to whom the companion reports, that is, who specifically in the congregation is the companion's primary contact person or group. Is it the board? The transition committee? The search committee when that is formed? Is the chair of any of these groups the primary contact or someone else?

- *Accountability.* The agreement should state clearly to whom the companion is accountable. Normally one is accountable to the congregation she serves, but since the companion also has ties to the judicatory, the contract should make clear to what extent this dual link may affect the companion's work. It is important that the companion not be seen as an agent of the judicatory, but the congregation should also realize that a companion does have a broader responsibility for the welfare of the congregation. The companion may therefore, under specified circumstances, including prior consultation with congregation authorities, refer problems that she is unable to deal with to the judicatory executive. It should be made clear that such cases should be extreme ones that threaten the integrity of the congregation's search.

- *Confidentiality.* The companion should agree to keep information about the congregation, the candidates, and anything else relating to the transition confidential, just as members of the board, transition committee, and search committee are expected to do.

- *Feedback and evaluation.* The companion should agree with the contact person (see above) on a procedure for periodic review and feedback on his work. This could range from a simple "How are we doing?" exchange after meetings to a formal checklist of issues for a whole committee to discuss with the companion.

- *Relationship with the new pastor and help with the start-up.* The transition process will be enhanced if the companion is expected to monitor the developing relationship of congregation and new pastor, from the formation of a letter of agreement through at least the first year of the new ministry. An agreement with the companion on general expectations for this period (e.g., recommendations on aspects of the welcome, helping set up a mutual ministry process and review, and suggestions for celebration) is desirable.

- *Communicating terms of agreement.* The congregation must agree to make all the individuals and groups with whom the companion will work aware of the nature of the companion's work and to encourage them to support it.

This list of contractual terms may seem daunting at first, but it should not deter a congregation from taking on the services of a transition companion. The process is certain to go more easily with a companion than going it alone, and the companion will be on hand to offer advice when difficulties arise. Companions tend to volunteer for their role because they are gracious, caring people who love the church and are motivated to do their bit to help it function well. Congregations that have used companions in their transitions are usually so pleased with them that they hold celebrations for them at the official end of the transition and remain fast friends with them afterwards.

Notes

This article is based in part on material written by H. I. "Dusty" Miller, an experienced transition companion. Used by permission.

1. There are strong arguments for paying a transition companion. Payment provides motivation for both companion and congregation to fulfill the terms of their commitment to each other throughout a transition and it symbolizes the value the church places on this service. However, other factors are at work. Many transition companions will be volunteers who willingly assume

the responsibility as a form of ministry. Family- or pastoral-size congregations with limited budgets may be hard pressed to justify payment for this service, particularly if they feel it should be provided by the judicatory. Payment may even hinder the interpersonal link between a companion and a congregation in transition by introducing a possible basis for conflict. In the case of family- or pastoral-size congregations, perhaps the companion should be reimbursed for travel or other expenses, but rewarded in other ways for his services; for example, by a reception or a contribution to a charity in the companion's honor. It is likely that larger congregations, of program or corporate size, will have both the finances and the readiness to accept the responsibility of paying a companion.

LEADERSHIP CHANGES DURING AND AFTER A PASTORAL TRANSITION

CONGREGATIONS TEND TO HAVE both active and passive members. The active members are those who provide the leadership and the majority of the financial support; the passive members participate in the congregation programs but are not significantly involved in planning or running them. The Alban Institute, in its seminars, refers to congregations A and B. Congregation A may include about 20 percent of the membership while supplying 80 percent of the leadership and financial support. Congregation B is the complementary image, providing about 80 percent of the membership but only 20 percent of the leadership and funding. The composition of these groups is likely to change in the course of a pastoral transition. The new pastor and congregation leaders would be well advised to learn about and respond to those changes as a new pastorate begins.

Congregation Structure Before a Transition

This structure becomes a matter to monitor if a long-term (10 years or more) pastorate is ending. In this case, congregation A has most likely come to reflect and value the age, theology, lifestyle, pastoral style, and political perspectives of their pastor. Members less attracted to the pastor's character-

istics (e.g., leaders from an earlier pastorate) have probably tended to withdraw to the fringes of the congregation, though perhaps remaining active in a program that adds meaning to their life (e.g., the choir or a prayer group in which they have bonded with other people).

This is a natural tendency, but one with potential for leadership challenges. A long pastorate offers stability and the potential to develop and realize long-term goals, but stability can develop into a resistance to change and a leadership group committed to the status quo. Members who have leadership potential but do not fit the congregation A model may not be offered leadership positions and, as a result, feel disenfranchised. The resignation of a long-term pastor can challenge an entrenched leadership structure, since a transition requires opening a congregation to the possibility, if not the need, for changes in the way it does things.

Structure During the Transition

A congregation that conducts a self-study in the discernment phase of the pastoral transition is well advised to present itself honestly and accurately in the profile that results. Now is the time to take steps to ensure that the whole membership is offered ways to participate meaningfully in creating a picture of who the congregation is and what it wants to become under a new pastor. There can be both risk and challenge in this task. The transition and search committees may have to reach out beyond the core of congregation A to members who have not taken an active leadership role in recent years. Unless care is taken to focus on the needs of the whole congregation and to represent the views of a wide range of individuals and subgroups, the picture of the congregation and the ministry description of a new pastor may be distorted. Some members may come to see that the congregation description does not fit them or show appreciation for what they do in it and leave.

The leadership, or congregation A, must therefore leave itself open to hearing about and considering views that may conflict with theirs. They can do this by including in their deliberations representatives of other views in the congregation. The presence or assistance of an outside monitor (e.g., judicatory representative or transition companion) can also help the congregation A leaders widen their thinking.

Structure in the New Pastorate

It is likely that the restructuring of the congregation will accelerate in the first year of the new pastorate. If the discernment process has been effective, the congregation will have a renewed sense of its identity and goals, and the new pastor will arrive eager to fulfill the perceived mandate of the search. There will naturally be some people who are fired up by the new goals and gravitate toward the new pastor's vision of how to attain them. There will be others, however, who are less enthusiastic, a group that may include many of the congregation A leaders. How can their enthusiasm be rekin-

dled? How can the tendency of the enthusiasts for the new regime to "go it alone" be restrained?

It will take conscious work by the new pastor and by the governing board, transition committee, and other groups in the congregation to educate themselves about the phenomenon and to open leadership widely to minimize feelings of disenfranchisement and domination. The pastor will be advised to go out of her way to get to know members and to encourage them to use their talents to fulfill a leadership or ministry role within the congregation. But the pastor will need the help of all well-meaning members in encouraging the development of a leadership group that reflects a broad spectrum of the congregation's membership, while learning about and affirming the roles that those outside the leadership group make.

A new pastorate will see congregations A and B that differ from those of the former pastorate. But these groups will not become fixed and mutually exclusive. Members will move in and out of leadership roles and change their levels and forms of congregational activity, as their interests and time commitments motivate them. Congregation A will still come to reflect and value the age, theology, lifestyle, pastoral style, and political perspectives of their pastor, but the pastor will encourage its members to be open to the participation of others with whom they may not agree. Likewise, congregation B will continue to represent a large majority of the congregation, but its members will not feel that their views and talents are unwanted or unappreciated by the congregation's leaders. The pastor in a family- or pastoral-size congregation and leaders and staff in larger ones will try to encourage and affirm all members in their chosen activity in a congregation, but seek a leadership that looks to change thoughtfully with the times.

TRANSITION IN MULTI-CONGREGATION LINKAGES

THERE HAS BEEN A LONG TRADITION of two or more congregations sharing a building, a pastor, or other features such as programs. The variety of linkages is great, and new ones appear constantly while older ones evolve as conditions change. The phenomenon of the parent congregation with a mission offshoot also has a long history. Sometimes, in small communities, two congregations of different denominations have reached an agreement to join in worship while retaining some separate denominational ties. In such cases, the joint congregation often selects its pastors alternately from the two denominations. More common nowadays are linkages within a denomination that allow smaller congregations to share one or more pastors and consolidate programs or liturgies while retaining separate facilities.

Pastoral transitions for linked congregations pose unique challenges for all involved in them: clergy, governing boards, judicatories, and transition companions. While it is not possible to cover all the different circumstances and challenges each linkage faces, some general comments may help. The most common feature of such transitions is the need to allow additional time for the increased number of interactions that the linkages necessitate, and, with this time, the related need for extra care, consideration, and especially communication in all these interactions. A variety of scenarios are possible; here are two examples.

A Union of Convenience

Two small congregations of the same denomination in adjoining communities that are both in serious population decline decided some years ago to share a pastor. Each congregation would continue to function independently of the other, except to arrange service schedules with the pastor and payment for pastoral services. The result was a succession of short-term pastorates, as the long-term prospects of the two congregations seemed bleak and it was unclear to whom the pastor was ultimately responsible. After a pastorate that was generally agreed to be a failure, the denomination's judicatory realized that a rescue-and-renewal operation was essential if either or both congregations were to survive, much less prosper. The judicatory believed the continued existence of these congregations essential to the denomination's presence in that area, but it saw the difficulties it faced in imposing a solution. Long-term survival and renewal required a mechanism to override the separateness of the congregations and make a longer pastorate possible.

First, some bitter feelings over the neglect of these congregations by the judicatory and the shortcomings of their latest pastor had to be aired so the congregations could move on. Second, the two congregations had to develop better communication to address their dilemma and agree to work together toward a solution. These two processes took a long time, with the assistance of the judicatory representative and a transition companion. The congregations could not cooperate in a search for another shared pastor until a number of issues that had never been addressed were identified and, very gradually, dealt with. The result, however, was at least a qualified success. The congregations faced up to their situations and formalized a relationship that promised not only to support and nurture their new joint pastor but also to enliven the congregations. In the process some powerful members who wanted to return to the old separate ways had to be confronted and either persuaded to join the common effort or be excluded from it. The defection of some of these figures, however, made possible a more participatory and outward-looking membership of both congregations. The resolution of this crisis thus not only revived the congregations and strengthened their relations with the judicatory, but also led to a viable and productive relationship.

A Cluster Ministry Evolves

A congregation in a declining inner-city area found its membership dropping drastically, while it retained a core of members and a large endowment. It sought new life in a cluster ministry, joining with two small congregations close to the city that, though largely rural, had become isolated by the development of industrial complexes. The three congregations essentially gave up their individual identities to become a single congregation, with a single governing body but three different sites for worship and programs. Three clergy served the grouping, and members moved freely among the sites, in the process developing relationships that crossed barriers of race, ethnicity, age, and residence. However, as the city congregation's area redefined itself and the congregation's decline was arrested, some of its members urged a break-up of the cluster and a return to independent congregation status. When a clergy retirement occurred and the two remaining clergy split on the issue of the break-up, the judicatory realized that a search for a third pastor could not be conducted until the issue of the future of the cluster was satisfactorily resolved.

The first challenge was how to set up a process to handle the issue. How could all the congregations share in governance of the cluster effectively when the inner-city congregation had more members and a large endowment? What, indeed, would enable the cluster to continue its life productively? The congregations, with the help of a judicatory representative, worked out an arrangement to form a working group that included a variety of members but an agreement to reach decisions by consensus rather than a majority vote, even a large one. This group met at all three congregation locations, listened to all who wanted to voice opinions and suggestions, and eventually concluded by renegotiating the terms of the cluster to give the inner-city church a larger voice in the cluster's decisions while retaining the agreement's basic features.

Reflections on the Examples

These stories suggest the kinds of situations that can generate linkages and the challenges that can develop within a linkage. Given the condition of mainline denominations nowadays, it is likely that numerous variations on them will arise. Thus denominations and congregations should look into the history of and recent developments in congregational linkages and prepare to take advantage of the benefits that linkages can offer while avoiding their many pitfalls. Pastoral transitions offer a point at which input from the judiciary can be both supportive of and appreciated by congregations uncertain about their future. A judicatory could serve both its own interests, and those of the congregations affected, by referring to successful instances of congregations in similar circumstances that decided to seek some formal linkage to facilitate a more secure future and a mission that extended beyond themselves.

The examples do not reflect the amount of time and work that reaching a satisfactory working arrangement entails. Many people, in the congregations and outside them, have to commit themselves to an arduous process. They must understand the kind of path they are committing themselves to in considering the formation of a cluster. A new process for exploring alternative structurings of a linkage must be developed in each instance with the active involvement of those most concerned, so that the process becomes their joint property. Patience is thus essential. There will also have to be extensive communication among a variety of participants, who may feel less comfortable away from their home turf. These discussions are a form of discernment about whether the Holy Spirit is calling a cluster into existence. If a cluster is agreed upon and a search process does eventually occur, all involved will have reached a high level of commitment to a joint cause and a clear understanding of a future they hope to realize.

The lengthy discernment process, such as those in the examples, probably should be followed by a clean break from existing practices (e.g., each congregation always having its own liturgy, service schedules, and programs) before the search process itself can begin. Worship and pastoral services will have to be arranged with the help of judiciary staff and other clergy in the area. The linked congregations need to experience working together in the new form of the relationship (e.g., with shared worship experiences, adult education or vacation Bible school, joint choirs, or shared social events), to develop trust and to see if any snags occur and work them out. It is likely that personnel changes in governing boards and officers have occurred in the interim, and these new leaders have to be integrated into the ongoing process.

A search committee with representatives of all congregations in the linkage should include people who have not burned out or lost credibility in the process to this point. It may be difficult to decide who is to preside over the search committee if two or more suitable candidates from different congregations offer their services. In that case, creative ways to use the talents of all these leaders must be sought.

It is probably a good idea to identify a person to serve as administrator of the search, communicate with all members of the group, and make arrangements for meetings, correspondence, travel, and so forth. This position carries heavy responsibilities. An administrator should be familiar with and have the confidence of the congregations involved. The administrator will need the authority to make the financial commitments the search involves. Arrangements for visits by candidates and their families to the linked congregations will also be more complex. A longer time for the visit will be necessary for the candidate and each congregation to become acquainted with one another.

Discernment processes that lead to multicongregation linkages of this type may help shape the future of mainline denominations. These processes may be complex and challenging, but at least no one will find them boring. Anyone involved in them, from judiciary staff or congregations, should be prepared to join in learning with all the other participants. All who participate in this activity are likely to experience the satisfaction of contributing to the well-being of their congregation and denomination and to renew their own faith and spiritual commitment.

ET 5

WHEN THE DEPARTING PASTOR
STAYS IN TOWN

IT USED TO BE that retiring or resigning pastors left the community when they left a congregation; many denominations even required it. Today, many clergy spouses have careers, an increasing number of clergy own their own homes, and many want to continue to live in the community that they have served and come to regard as their hometown. In these cases, it is important to find ways the departing pastor can remain in the community, even as a member of the congregation, in a way that makes the experience positive for all. While it is clear that a former pastor should in no way interfere in the affairs of the congregation he formerly served, it is important that pastors, and their families, not be isolated from friends and a church home they have loved.

The farewell activities (see PT 4) and liturgies at the end of a pastorate (see ET 9; ET 10) can help members of a congregation to end a pastoral relationship while still maintaining ties of friendship with the departing pastor and family. But more is needed when the departing pastor will remain in town. The board and the departing pastor need to create clear guidelines for the departing pastor's participation as a member of the congregation. This agreement must be shared with members of the congregation and interim pastor. The

search committee can also present it to candidates for pastor and ultimately it can be included as a part of the signed call agreement.

Development of the agreement will be smoothest with the early participation of the judicatory executive or staff member. That person can meet privately with the departing pastor (and spouse) soon after the resignation is announced and discuss what the pastor is planning or wishes to do. An advantage of an early private meeting is the opportunity to work with the pastor before anyone else is involved, to correct misperceptions, establish boundaries, and so on. If the pastor has been intending or hoping to do certain things that might be inappropriate (e.g., offering to preach on a regular basis, or conduct baptisms, weddings, or funerals for former members) the judicatory representative can say in a loving way, in private, "Now, let's think about that," and help the pastor discover the lack of wisdom in such a plan.

After this initial meeting, the judicatory representative should meet with the board to discuss the formulation of a written agreement that will spell out terms for the departing pastor's participation in the congregation. This agreement should reflect concern and fairness for the interim, the new pastor, and the congregation, as well as the departing pastor. When complete, this document should be approved by the judicatory, board, and departing pastor and shared with the interim pastor and congregation (so members will understand the kinds of participation in congregational life that are appropriate for a departing pastor). Such an agreement should include the following:

- An explanation of why the departing pastor wants to maintain membership in the congregation.
- A statement that the departing pastor and new pastor will affirm one another's ministry, and not undermine those ministries in any way. This means that the departing pastor will not interfere with the work of the new pastor in any way nor join with those who have complaints about the successor's ministry. The departing pastor will be supportive of the new pastor's style of ministry and objectives. At the same time, the new pastor will refrain from criticism of things that have been done in the past.
- A statement that the departing pastor will not initiate contacts with members of the congregation for purposes of pastoral care.
- A commitment from the pastor and spouse to absent themselves from the congregation for at least one year— from worship, fellowship occasions, official meetings, and the like. In addition, if the clergy spouse has been an employee of the congregation, the spouse should resign from that position.
- The procedure to be followed with funerals and weddings; meaning, the former pastor will not officiate at such services. The former pastor may assist at the request of the family and at the invitation of the interim or the new pastor. Under no circumstances should the former pastor initiate contact upon a bereavement or notice of a wedding.

The interim pastor and, later, the new pastor should invite the departing pastor to meet to discuss the agreement, to be sure that they agree in their understanding of it and of their obligations under it. It is the responsibility of the interim or new pastor to initiate this meeting, since the departing pastor has agreed to be absent from functions of the congregation; initiating such contact could be interpreted as interference on the part of the departing pastor. It will be most helpful if a skilled third party is present at this conversation to ensure that each individual involved hears clearly what the other is saying and that points of ambiguity are surfaced and explored. This third party can consistently summarize and repeat the points that have been agreed upon by the two parties, and be responsible for having both parties sign the written agreement. If the pastors want to revise the agreement in any way, the revision should be made in writing and approved by the board, and the judicatory executive must also add her signature to the new agreement.

If the departing pastor, interim, new pastor, or congregation fails to meet any of the expectations, any of the parties should be free to identify the infraction and ask that a resolution process begin. The board should work with the individuals involved toward a solution that will be compassionate and constructive and will not damage individuals or the congregation. If necessary, someone from the judicatory staff should be involved in the solution.

Pastors who continue to live in the community they served and the members of their congregations both have to learn to live into their new roles with each other. Since it is easy to continue behaving in old ways, intentional training in adjusting to the new relationship is essential to make the new relationship work. Having a formal agreement will help both the departing pastor and congregation's members to realize how necessary it is for them to say farewell to the pastoral relationship that has existed between them. A successful reorientation of these roles can produce benefits for all concerned, congregation and departing and active clergy. The pastor who has left can get to know members of the congregation in different ways and, in time, as the new pastor feels confident that the new relationship is truly in effect, can assist the new pastor in ways the pastor can direct. Retired clergy, particularly, can have an opportunity for personal growth and service in the community they have served before.

Note

Material for this article was drawn from a parish ministry retirement model developed by William S. Ryan and Narka K. Ryan when they served as interim regional ministers for the Christian Church (Disciples of Christ) in Virginia, and is used by permission.

SAMPLE QUESTIONS
FOR EXIT CONVERSATIONS

1. What do you consider your most important accomplishments in this congregation?

2. What will you miss most about this place and this ministry?

3. What are you not going to miss?

4. Were there things you had hoped to do but were not able to accomplish?

5. Describe one incident you handled well that you might use as a model in the future.

6. Describe one incident you managed poorly and wish you could do over again.

7. What dreams have you seen realized, and which will you have to relinquish as you leave?

8. Name five people on whose lives you feel you have made a significant impact.

9. Describe at least two critical points in the life of the congregation where you feel you made the right decision and took the risk of convincing this congregation to follow you.

10. Can you think of a point where you made the wrong decision and wish you had decided differently?

11. What in this ministry took the heaviest toll on your body and spirit?

12. What were the things that always seemed to refresh your spirit?

13. How did this congregation bless you and your family? (Optional question for single clergy: How did the congregation support and affirm you as a single person?)

14. How was this congregation hard on your family? (How was it difficult for this congregation to support you as a single person?)

15. During your tenure here, was there any time when you felt this congregation really let you down? Describe why you felt that way. To what degree have you recovered from that experience?

16. As you think of the future of this congregation, what would you say is its unrealized potential?

17. What will be some of the difficult challenges your successor will have to face?

18. Who are some of the people you will miss most?

19. Who are the people who will have difficulty seeing you leave?

20. Have you made a list of things you have normally taken care of that someone will have to be responsible for during the transition? If no, how and when will you make it?

21. Is there anything you want to add?

ET 7

SURVEY QUESTIONS
FOR A CONGREGATION PROFILE

WHETHER A SURVEY is completed in writing or in an open-space activity, it should produce information that will present an accurate picture of the congregation. In addition to the questions that follow, written questions can be framed (with multiple-choice answers, so collating the information is as quick as possible) to gather information such as age, marital status, educational level, numbers and ages of children. Even if an open-space activity is used, the committee might also decide to include some of the questions below in a written survey.

1. How many years have you been a member of this congregation?
   a. 1 year or less
   b. 2 to 4 years
   c. 5 to 10 years
   d. more than 10 years

2. How many years have you been a member of this denomination?
   a. not a member of this denomination
   b. 3 years or less
   c. 4 to 10 years
   d. More than 10 years. Those in corner (d) might be asked to raise a hand if they are lifetime members of the denomination.

3. How far do you live from the church?
   a. within walking distance
   b. a 5-minute drive or less
   c. a 5- to 15-minute drive
   d. more than a 15-minute drive.

4. Which describes your family composition?
   a. no children
   b. dependent children
   c. empty nest

5. If you answered *b* to the previous question, what are the ages of your children? (Stand according to the age of your youngest child.)
   a. preschool
   b. elementary school
   c. middle school or high school
   d. college

6. How would you describe your employment situation?
   a. employed full time
   b. employed part time
   c. not working outside home
   d. retired

7. Which service do you regularly attend? (Fill in local options.)

8. Do you spend at least 20 minutes a day in prayer?
   a. no
   b. yes

9. Do you read scripture every day?
   a. no
   b. yes

10. Do you tithe (give at least 10 percent of all you earn to church and charity)?
    a. no
    b. yes

11. Do you ask a blessing at a family meal?
    a. no
    b. yes

12. Do you regularly attend a weekly adult group for prayer, Bible study, or discussion of issues, in addition to Sunday worship?
    a. no
    b. yes

13. Three years from now, would you like the congregation to be:
    a. its current size?
    b. 10 percent larger?
    c. 50 percent larger?
    d. twice as large?

14. If you had to pick between the following, do you think it is more important in the next five years for us to grow in:
    a. numbers?
    b. spiritual depth?
    c. social action or social justice?
    d. the way our members minister to one another?

15. Do we do an adequate job serving both the spiritual and other needs of our immediate neighborhood or community?
    a. no
    b. yes

16. Which is our congregation better known for?
    a. music ministries
    b. educational ministries

17. Which would you prefer we be known for?
    a. music
    b. education

18. With regard to our physical facilities, do you think:
    a. our physical facilities are adequate and in good shape?
    b. we need to spruce things up and possibly add certain facilities?
    c. major improvements are necessary?

19. Do you think we do a good job integrating new members?
    a. no
    b. yes

20. How would you describe participation in the work of the congregation?
    a. Our volunteer base is broad and deep enough.
    b. The same few do most of the work in our congregation.

21. Is our congregation open and affirming to gay or lesbian persons?
    a. yes
    b. no
    c. not sure

22. Should our congregation be open and affirming to gay or lesbian persons?
    a. yes
    b. no

23. Would you attend a new weekly worship with contemporary music (keyboard, guitar, and drums)?
    a. no
    b. yes

24. Would you like to see such a service offered, even if you were not likely to attend?
    a. no
    b. yes

25. Are you interested in having a regular healing service?
    a. no
    b. yes

26. We would like to have a pastor who is outstanding at both preaching and pastoral care. If we had to choose between these skills, which would you pick?
    a. strong preaching
    b. pastoral care

27. Would you prefer the pastor to be a better:
    a. manager?
    b. leader?
    (Leaders are skilled at developing a vision and communicating it to others. Managers can take someone else's good idea and turn it into a reality. It is unusual for clergy to be good at both.)

28. Would you prefer our new pastor to be:
    a. under 40?
    b. 40 to 55?
    c. over 55?
    d. Age does not matter.

29. If you had to pick between them, would you prefer our new pastor to be skilled in:
    a. evangelism?
    b. social action and social justice work?

30. Is it more important to you that your new pastor be:
    a. well educated and intellectually challenging?
    b. warm, friendly, and gregarious?

31. If you had to choose, would you prefer your new pastor be:
    a. good with children?
    b. good with seniors?

32. Would you prefer your new pastor to be:
    a. good at stirring things up?
    b. good at calming things down?

33. Would you prefer a pastor who represents:
    a. an orthodox point of view with regard to our denominational tradition?
    b. a more eclectic and ecumenical theology?

34. What do you prefer for gender of our next pastor?
    a. male
    b. female
    c. Gender does not make a difference as long as the most competent person is chosen.

ET 8

QUESTIONS FOR REFLECTION ON THE TRANSITION PROCESS

THE CONGREGATION WILL HAVE DONE a great deal of work in the course of the transition process. It would be a shame for this work to go unreported and end without reflection. The groups and individuals who made significant contributions to the transition should be shown that what they did is known and understood. The information about the transition that is gathered will serve as a resource not only for the congregation in question but also for the judicatory and others concerned with transitions.

Therefore, it will be a good idea for groups such as the transition committee, governing board, search committee, and individuals such as the chairs of these committees and the transition companion (if one was used), to be interviewed and the responses kept in a permanent record. The judicatory may suggest this exercise and offer assistance in organizing it, but if they do not, the transition companion, transition committee, or board should assume responsibility. The interviewer and recorder may come from the congregation, or volunteers may be sought from other congregations. The setting of the interviews should be informal enough to encourage frank discussion. It would be most helpful to all concerned to report both successes and things that did not go as well as they might have.

The following list of questions, arranged by types of information, should guide the interviews. They can be selected or amended to address particular circumstances. Note that these questions first ask someone to provide some facts about their experience in a transition, but then go on to solicit comment on that experience. The comments are the important part. A digest of the significant insights that the comments reveal will be a valuable resource.

1. Describing the involvement of the individual or committee:
   a. Please tell us what you did in the transition.
   b. Did your work take the time you thought it might, or more or less?
   c. What in your work brought you the greatest satisfaction?
   d. What did you enjoy most?
   e. What was the least satisfying or enjoyable aspect of your work?
   f. Did your work affect your spiritual life? If so, how?
   g. Was your work hampered in any way? If so, describe.

2. Reflecting on the role of transition companion or consultant in the transition process:
   a. Was such a resource used in your transition? (If yes, continue this section.)

b. Describe ways in which this person was helpful in the process.

c. Were there ways the person could have been more helpful? Describe them.

d. From this experience, would you want to use, or would you recommend, a companion or consultant in a future search or other situation?

e. Do you think you would be interested in serving in a companion's role elsewhere with suitable training? Please comment.

3. Reflecting on the process:

a. From your experience of the transition, did the process go smoothly?

b. If anything did not go smoothly, describe the situation and its outcome.

c. Were you, as an individual or committee member, faced with a conflict? Describe the situation, its outcome, your involvement in the conflict. Do you think the conflict was resolved (if it was) satisfactorily? If it was resolved well, how did that happen?

4. Miscellaneous questions:

a. Experience with the middle judicatory:

• Did you have any experience with the judicatory or its representatives in your work in the transition? (Continue if yes.)

• What did they do? Describe one or more helpful actions.

• Would you have liked any additional help? If so, what would you have liked?

• How clear and useful were materials the judicatory provided?

• Did you have easy access to your judicatory executive or staff at critical times in the transition? Please comment.

b. Relationship with the congregation:

• Did your service in the transition period affect your relationship with the congregation? If so, how?

• Were you or your committee able to reflect the diversity of the congregation and the range of views in it? Please comment.

c. Advice and future service:

• Do you have any advice for anyone serving in your position in a transition? If so, what?

• Would you agree to serve in your role in another transition? Why or why not?

• Would you prefer to serve in another role? If so, what and why?

ET 9

A Ritual for Ending a Pastorate

THIS RITUAL USUALLY TAKES PLACE at the conclusion of the Sunday morning service. It symbolizes the relinquishing of pastoral authority by the departing pastor, while allowing the pastor to maintain links of friendship with its individual members of the congregation. It is particularly appropriate when a pastor will continue to live in the community. (For additional suggestions when the pastor remains in the community, see ET 5.)

The pastoral office can often be symbolized by items that represent pastoral authority, including the Bible, Eucharistic vessels, keys to the church building, a gavel (if the pastor presided over governing board meetings), and vestments. The symbolic items (excluding the vestments, which the pastor is wearing) are placed on the altar and selected members of the congregation are invited forward to receive them. Thus the symbols of pastoral authority are returned to the members of the congregation, to be retained by them until a new pastor has accepted the call to this congregation. These items may, within a service of installation, be handed to the congregation's new pastor.

With the handing over of each item, the departing pastor may share a word or two about its significance in her life and to the congregation's life. Once they are all handed over, the chairperson of the governing board says:

We accept these items of pastoral authority from you. We thank you for using them wisely and well while you were our pastor. We will hold them in sacred trust until they can be given to a new pastor who will come to serve us.

With the help of one or two members of the congregation, the pastor can remove the vestments she is wearing while still in the sanctuary. They should then be hung in an appropriate place or placed on the altar. Should the departing pastor now be in shirtsleeves, someone can help her put on a suit jacket. Those who received the symbols of pastoral authority should place these items on the altar or on a table near the hanging vestments. They should then accompany the pastor, dressed in street clothes, to the entrance of the church, where members of the congregation will say farewell.

Greeting members of the congregation at the door in street clothes symbolizes the fact that the pastor has given up all pastoral authority in this congregation and now is simply a friend. This ceremony helps people realize they should not ask their former pastor to return to conduct a baptism, wedding, or funeral. The pastoral relationship is over. A new pastor will have the authority for such rites in the future.

ET 10

A SERVICE FOR ENDING
A PASTORAL RELATIONSHIP

P *presiding minister*   R *response of departing pastor*   C *congregation or people*

SERVICE OF THE WORD

1. An opening hymn may be sung. The people stand.

P Blessed be God, Creator, Redeemer, and Holy Spirit.
C **Blessed be God's reign, now and forever. Amen.**

P There is one Body and one Spirit;
C **There is one hope in God's call to us;**

P One Lord, one Faith, one Baptism;
C **One God and Parent of all.**

P The Lord be with you.
C **And also with you.**

P Let us pray.

Almighty and everlasting God, by whose Spirit the whole body of your faithful people is governed, receive our prayers, which we offer to you for all members of your holy Church, that in their ministry they may faithfully serve you. Direct us, O Lord, in all our doings with your most gracious favor, and further us with your continual help; that in all our works begun, continued, and ended in you, we may glorify your Name. We pray for the holy catholic Church. Fill it with truth and peace. Where it is corrupt, purify it; where it is in error, direct it; where in anything it is amiss, reform it. Where it is right, strengthen it; where it is in want, provide for it; where it is divided, reunite it; for the sake of Jesus Christ our Lord. Amen.

THE MINISTRY OF THE WORD

2. Any of the following may be read.

First Reading

Genesis 31:44-46, 48-49, 50b
The Lord watch between you and me when we are absent one from another

Genesis 12:1-9
Abraham's departure from Haran and God's promise to bless him

Deuteronomy 18:15-18
God will raise up a prophet like Moses

Deuteronomy 32:1-9
The farewell of Moses

Joshua 24:1, 14-25
Joshua's farewell to his people

Ecclesiastes 3:1-7; 7:8, 10, 13-14
A time for everything; better the end than the beginning

Second Reading

1 Corinthians 3:4-11
Paul planted, Apollos watered, God gave growth

Acts 16:9-10
Paul's call to Macedonia

Acts 20:17-22, 25-28, 32, 36-38b
Paul's apologia for his ministry at Ephesus

1 Thessalonians 5:12-25
Paul encourages the ministry among the Thessalonians

2 Thessalonians 2:13—3:5
Paul gives thanks for the success of the gospel

Philippians 4:1-10, 23
Rejoice in the Lord always

Gospel

Matthew 9:35-38
The harvest is plentiful but the laborers are few

Matthew 25:31-40
As you did it to the least of these you did it to me

Luke 12:35-38
The faithful servant

Luke 17:7-10
We are unworthy servants; we have only done our duty

John 10:14-18
The ministry of the good shepherd

John 21:15-19
Feed my sheep

Sermon

3. *It may be appropriate for the judicatory executive to preach the sermon in the course of which a charge should be given to the congregation concerning the nature of ministry.*

Apostles' Creed

4. *The departing pastor then addresses these words to the congregation:*

R   On *[date,]* I began ministry in this congregation. I have, with God's help and to the best of my abilities, exercised this trust. After prayer and careful consideration, it now seems to me that I should leave this charge, and I publicly state that my tenure as pastor of this church ends this day.

5. *The pastor may, if desired, briefly state his/her plans for the future.*

6. *The executive says:*

   Do you, the people of *[this church,]* recognize and accept the end of this pastoral relationship?

C   **We do.**

7. *Then the pastor may express thanksgiving for the time of tenure, with its joys and sorrows, and state hopes for the future of the congregation.*

8. *The pastor may present to officers of the congregation a letter of resignation, the keys to the church, or other symbols fitting to the occasion.*

9. *The pastor may be joined by members of the family who may want to express what life in the congregation has meant to them.*

10. *Representatives of the congregation may wish to respond to the pastor and family, and bid them Godspeed.*

11. *The executive may then indicate what provision has been made for continuation of the ministries of the parish.*

12. *The departing pastor and the congregation then say together the following prayer:*

C   **O God, you have bound us together for a time as pastor and people to work for the advancement of your kingdom in this place. We give you thanks for the ministry which we have shared in these years now past.**

   Silence

C   **We thank you for your patience with us despite our blindness and slowness of heart. We thank you for your forgiveness and mercy in the face of our many failures.**

   Silence

C Especially we thank you for your never-failing presence with us through these years, and for the deeper knowledge of you and of each other which we have attained.

Silence

C We thank you for those who have been joined to this part of Christ's family through baptism. We thank you for opening our hearts and minds again and again to your Word, and for feeding us abundantly with the Sacrament of the Body and Blood of your son.

Silence

C Now, we pray, be with those who leave and with those who stay; and grant that all of us, by drawing nearer to you, may always be close to each other in the communion of saints. All this we ask for the sake of Jesus Christ, your Son, our Lord. Amen.

R The peace of the Lord be always with you.

C And also with you.

MINISTRY OF THE SACRAMENT

13. If the Lord's Supper is to follow, the service continues with the offertory.

14. After the Communion:

C Almighty God, we thank you for feeding us with the Body and Blood of your Son and for uniting us with Him in the fellowship of your Holy Spirit. We thank you for raising up among us faithful servants of your Word and Sacraments. We thank you especially for the work of *[pastor's name]* among us, (and the presence of *[his/her]* family here). Grant that both *[he/she]* and we may serve you in the days ahead, and always rejoice in your glory, and come at length into your heavenly kingdom; through Jesus Christ our Lord. Amen.

CHARGE AND BENEDICTION

Note

This service is modeled after an Episcopal service and has been revised for ecumenical use.

PART 3

CLERGY EXPERIENCING TRANSITION

CT 1

SURVIVING A FAREWELL

ELISABETH KÜBLER-ROSS DESCRIBES DEATH as the final stage of growth.[1] Death provides us with that final opportunity to come to terms with our relationships, our values, and our lives. The process of grieving the death of a loved one, if approached with openness and vulnerability, also provides a growth opportunity. But being open and vulnerable is hard work and it feels uncomfortable, so we often deny that we will die and avoid grieving the deaths of loved ones. In death and grief, we need not so much protection from painful experience as the boldness to face it. If we choose to love, we must also have the courage to grieve.

The end of a pastor's relationship with a congregation offers the same opportunities for learning and growth and also the same temptations for avoidance and denial that a death does. Thus the manner in which clergy close out a ministry can model the way they plan for their own death and help others to face theirs. Clergy should ask themselves, as they prepare to end a pastorate, "Is this how I want to die?" and "Is this how I want to support people as they face their deaths?" If the answers are no, some changes are needed.

Many pastors rightly assume that the end of a pastorate will involve pain, so their approach is to rush through it as fast as they can. This manic behavior, clearly a death-denying approach to closing out one's life in a pastorate, has the advantage of avoiding pain, but at a cost. It might seem that avoiding the most painful parts would ease the transition, but in fact pastor and congregation are left with powerful emotions they have not dealt with. It is not possible to force powerful feelings deep inside while painting a smile on one's face. Unexpressed and unacknowledged emotions will emerge, possibly in unexpected ways, and neither pastor nor congregation will come out of the experience feeling whole or good about themselves. Nor will they be prepared to enter into new relationships in a new setting or with a new pastor.

In a study of clergy termination styles related to its Pastorate Start-Up Project, the Alban Institute tried to understand the entire clergy transition process. It found that the grief process of clergy and congregation had direct relevance to the subsequent start-up process; certain *termination emotions* were found to be central to the transition experience.

Alban discovered that congregations that had not experienced a good termination process retained unresolved issues when a new pastor arrived. Sometimes a congregation was incapable of accepting new pastoral leadership; in such cases the new pastor became an unintended interim who left soon afterwards, frustrated, hurt, and disappointed. Other congregations found it difficult to make sound decisions when selecting a new pastor after a poor termination. Likewise, some clergy who arrived at their new congregation with unresolved feelings about leaving the last one began to feel depressed and discouraged, finding it hard to become energized with their new ministry.

Termination Tasks

John Fletcher, former president of Inter-Met Seminars, has concluded from studying terminally ill patients that such patients have four major tasks to perform when they learn they will die soon:

- taking control of what remains of their life;
- getting their affairs in order;
- letting old grudges go;
- thanking those to whom they are grateful.

Fletcher suggests that it is a clergyperson's calling to help terminally ill people to do these tasks. It is equally important for clergy to attend to these tasks when they plan their own departure from a congregation. For clergy, the tasks entail the following.

Taking Control

Clergy should actively bring closure to their ministries by developing a plan of action and a timetable for it. They can develop a schedule for seeing, phoning, or dropping notes to significant individuals, and for stopping in to say good-bye to various groups in the congregation.

Getting Affairs in Order

The affairs of the congregation should be in good shape for the next pastor. This means being sure that congregation records are up-to-date, that files have been cleaned out and updated, and that personal items have been removed from the church.

It also involves drawing up a list of things the pastor has done regularly, so they can be done in the interim period.

Letting Go of Old Grudges

A pastor cannot move on to a new congregation without putting the former one behind. A pastor should aim to resolve any conflict and reconcile with the other party. While this may not always be possible, the pastor who makes the effort can be freed of the burden of unexpressed feelings.

Saying Thank You

Thanking people can involve more than just saying thank you. The pastor should share both joys and disappointments with the people who are close. Saying thank you also involves offering a blessing: a pastor can affirm what is unique in people and tell them how much they have meant both personally and in ministry. In a final sermon, the pastor can bless the congregation in a similar way, by calling to their attention and thanking them for the good things they have shared together.

A Fifth Task

A fifth task, telling people the reasons for leaving, can be added for clergy to Fletcher's list. Many people in the congregation may wonder why the pastor is leaving: they need to know that the pastor's departure is not caused by something they did or did not do (unless, of course, that is the case). Members' feelings of sadness, guilt, emptiness, and loneliness at this time can be heightened by self-doubt if they feel that the pastor is leaving because of their actions. Members will be relieved to learn that a pastor needs to move away to experience personal and professional growth, or that the pastor has found the role he has been seeking for some time.

It may be helpful for a pastor to bring in an outsider, for example, a fellow member of the clergy, to serve as a consultant for the closure period. This person might help the pastor gain control over the departure and think through each step of leave-taking, pointing out the consequences of taking or not taking certain actions. Questions a consultant might ask the departing pastor include:

- How do you plan to tell the congregation you are leaving?
- How long will you stay after announcing your resignation?
- How will you decide a timetable for what you do in the remaining time?
- How you will say good-bye to people who have meant a lot to you?
- How will you deal with people who have hampered your ministry?
- How will you tell the congregation about your joys and disappointments here?
- About what matters will you and your family feel grief and anxiety? How will you deal with it?
- How will you encourage people to tell you candidly about your strengths and weaknesses as their pastor?

The consultant can serve as a sounding board for any feelings of anger or hostility that the pastor may have toward the congregation or a part of it, and can also help the pastor see how much the congregation has enriched her life.

The consultant can also advise the congregation, especially one grieving the loss of a beloved pastor, how best to express their feelings as they say farewell (see PT 4). The consultant can remind both pastor and congregation that farewells are most meaningful if they are balanced between praise and appreciation and realistic recognition of the ups and downs of the relationship.

Modeling Closure for a Congregation

Modeling is an important form of ministry, along with guidance, instruction, and exhortation. And there are too few good models in our "denial of death" society, a culture whose attitudes and practices work against effective closures. As a final act of ministry, then, a pastor can model ways of ending relationships by the way the pastor bids the congregation farewell. A pastor modeling termination for a congregation should be able to let go and to be open about the feelings that letting go generates. Doing this helps others let out their own feelings in farewells, and helps all learn to face death, the final stage of growth. The pastor who says farewell effectively has done a service to the congregation and to himself.

Modeling effective closure requires one to live deeply into many forms of death: the death of relationships, roles, functions, responsibilities, and the pastor-congregation link. As departing clergy think about the many "deaths" that they will experience because of their leaving, they might discover that sometimes it can be harder to let go of the pastor role than of the people themselves. Dying to the congregation, however, means dying to the role of its pastor. Failure to die this death often results in clergy feeling tempted to continue serving as the congregation's pastor and get involved with pastoral acts after they have left. Clergy should not try to become immortal by being indispensable to their congregants forever.

Notes

This article is based on Roy M. Oswald, *Running Through the Thistles* (Washington, D.C.: The Alban Institute, 1978). Copyright © 1978 the Alban Institute, Inc. Used by permission.

1.   Elisabeth Kübler-Ross, *Death: The Final Stage of Growth* (Englewood Cliffs, N.J.: Prentice-Hall, 1975).

CT 2

COPING WITH THE STRESS OF TRANSITION

SOME CONSIDER STRESS to be the number one killer in the Western world. Obituaries do not cite stress as a cause of death, but rather mention such things as heart attack, stroke, and accidents in which stress is a contributing factor. Stress enters our lives in situations of social readjustment, when we must depart from the familiar and predictable and confront the new and different. A pastor (and family) making the transition between congregations find themselves in a situation that can be highly stressful. Each family member faces his or her own particular stresses in making adjustments, and that can in turn create stresses for one another. While unmarried clergy do not have to help a family cope with stress, they lack a source of continuity and stability that may help reduce stress in their lives.

Departing from what is familiar and predictable, being confronted with the unexpected, triggers the fight-flight response in one's body. Like those of wild animals, our bodies react to the unexpected by getting ready to either fight or run: the heart beats faster, blood pressure rises, the pupils of the eyes dilate, the liver dumps sugar into the blood stream for quick energy, and the stomach stops digesting food. Without any thought, the body is ready for all the unpredictable things that may happen. Clergy in a new setting need to make con-

stant readjustments to the people and situations they encounter; they may push themselves to make a good first impression and strive to do everything right. As a result, they may be in a fight-flight state all day. These clergy often return home exhausted after a full day. Even with a good night's sleep, they may have trouble getting out of bed in the morning, because their bodies have not recovered from the stress of the days before.

While some people seem to thrive on such a stimulating life, many do not. At some point, their bodies may let them down, allowing a major illness to develop. They have played a game of brinksmanship with their bodies, unaware of the toll their drive has taken on them.

Identifying Stress and the Possibility of Illness

Thomas H. Holmes and Richard H. Rahe of the University of Washington School of Medicine worked with more than 5,000 patients,[1] studying the relationship between social readjustments (life events that require one to confront something new and depart from the familiar and predictable) and illness. To measure the level of social readjustments a person has made in a year, they developed a "Life Changes" inventory;

Roy Oswald has adapted their early social readjustment scale to relate specifically to the lives of clergy. The Clergy Life Changes Rating Scale (at the end of this article) can help clergy and their family members to recognize the variety of social adjustments they have had to make; the higher the score on this survey, the more likely it is that someone will experience physical illness. It is important for a new pastor to realize the effects that stress can have, and to take steps to recognize stress and reduce it before illness becomes a problem. In the long run, a healthy pastor who practices good stewardship of his own body can be a more effective leader in the congregation than one who does not.

While the life changes survey indicates by an increasing score that illness is becoming more likely, a second survey, the Strain Response, developed by John D. Adams,[2] can help identify whether the cumulative effects of strain are in fact taking a toll on the body. Adams's survey (a revised form of which is found at the end of the article) focuses on physical symptoms that can be precursors or indications of actual illness, and helps the user evaluate how she is dealing with stress. When clergy take these two surveys, they can become more aware of the events that are creating stress in their lives, as well as the physical manifestations that stress may be producing.

Coping Strategies to Reduce Stress

Whether an individual is feeling slightly stressed or completely stressed out, there are concrete coping strategies that can help lower one's stress level. Some of the generally well-known strategies are described briefly, while those that are less common are discussed in more detail.

Spiritual Formation

A deeper spiritual life will decrease stress. Jesus promised, "Come to me, all you that are weary and are carrying heavy burdens, and I will give you rest. Take my yoke upon you, and learn from me; for I am gentle and humble in heart, and you will find rest for your souls. For my yoke is easy, and my burden is light" (Matt. 11:28-30). A deep and abiding faith and trust in God can be an anchor of stability in a sea of flux. This faith is a constant we can return to at any time. When we move into prayer, our burdens are lightened or lifted from us. The familiarity and predictability of a Christian worship ritual can also transport us into the everlasting arms of God. Familiar hymns sung with people we know and trust can also bring swift relief.

One must regularly set aside time for prayer and scripture reading in order to develop a deeper spiritual life. We sometimes hear spiritual teachers describe spiritual discipline as "wasting time with God." Those who take time each day to waste time with God will find their stress levels decreasing.

Letting-Go Techniques

A variety of letting-go techniques have proven their value in reducing stress. Mastering all of them is not necessary; getting just one to work for you is enough. They include:

Meditation Many people think of meditation as a spiritual activity, but stress centers across the country teach it as a potent antidote to stress. Since meditation requires keeping one's mind totally in the here and now, focused on a relaxing place or image, the mind is prevented from reviewing the past or worrying about the future. When the mind is so focused, there is nothing to be stressed about—there is just you and the moment. The key to achieving and maintaining this focus is to repeat a word like *peace* or *calmness* or *quiet rest,* in time with one's breath. Research has shown that the stress level of those who meditate even 20 minutes a day is lower than the nonmeditator's; this effect lasts for hours. Longitudinal studies of those who meditate find that their health age is as much as 10 years younger than their chronological age.[3]

But meditation can be more than just a stress-reducing activity. For centuries, Christians of the Alexandrian tradition have used apophatic, or contemplative, prayer as a way of listening to God. This differs from the Roman tradition of prayer, with which we are more familiar, in which believers talk to God. Two things are necessary to turn meditation into prayer: intention (do you intend to be in contact with God during the meditative time?) and the use of a sacred word or phrase repeated in time with one's breath, which constantly brings images of God to the meditator. For this, some people use one of the many names of God; for example, Jehovah, Yahweh, Adonai, Elohim, or simply "O God." Other people use a line of scripture, such as "Be still and know that I am God" (Ps. 46:10). *Kyrie eleison,* Greek for "Lord have mercy," is thought to be the earliest Christian mantra. Those who are interested in learning more about this form of prayer are referred to works of Thomas Keating[4] and Basil Pennington.[5]

Biofeedback Biofeedback has been a major breakthrough in stress-reduction technology. It usually involves the monitoring of a bodily function such as blood pressure, hand temperature, and brain waves, in a way that allows the participant to see changes in these functions. Most biofeedback devices on the market are too expensive for individual use. One affordable alternative is Bio-Dots, small dots about the diameter of a pencil that are attached to the hand. They relate the degree of stress to hand temperature (cold hands are a sign of high stress) by becoming one of seven colors. If people wear a Bio-Dot on their watch hand, they can notice the color every time they look at their watch, and so judge the state of stress or relaxation in their body.[6]

Autogenic Training High-powered executives learn autogenic training to help them manage the stress of corporate life. Using a process of self-hypnosis that relaxes parts of the body one at a time, people learn to move their entire body into a deeply relaxed state within a few minutes. Fifteen minutes of this deeply relaxed state is the equivalent of an hour's sleep. People need to be trained by a professional to make this work for them.

Increasing One's Support Network Studies have shown that the immune system of those who belong to ongoing support groups is healthier than that of those who do not. Simply being with a group of people with whom one feels safe to share anything has a tremendous therapeutic effect.

Most of us think a good support network happens by luck or accident. Most often support takes hard work, but any effort to increase the quality of support in your life will have far-reaching effects on both your self-help and effectiveness at work. Some fortunate clergy move into a new community and are invited into a helpful clergy support group. Be aware, however, that clergy support groups often do not work well; casual gatherings of clergy often degenerate into complaint or bragging sessions, which will not help reduce stress.[7]

A pastor who is not now in a viable peer support group can try to identify another clergy member in the area with whom the pastor would be willing to share personal concerns. If that person is open and willing to begin a peer support group, the two can discuss two or three other people with whom they might want to form a group. (The Alban Institute has discovered that ecumenical groups are more successful in developing a high level of trust than same-denomination groups.)

Once the larger group is gathered, its members can explore hiring a facilitator to serve until the level of trust develops enough for members to manage on their own. An ideal facilitator should have competence in managing group processes, sensitivity to the complexities of pastoral work (thus some experience as a pastor is an asset), and "safety" (the inability to affect the career path of anyone in the group). Since a skilled facilitator should be paid, the participants will have to arrange the financing. A quality support group is worth paying for. Clergy should feel free to utilize their continuing education funds for this purpose.

Kinesthetic Spirituality

Kinesthetic spirituality engages the whole body. Such practices include Native American dance, the practices of the Shaker community and Sufi Muslims ("whirling dervishes"), Tai Chi, Hatha Yoga, as well as some forms of worship of African American and some charismatic Christian groups. For the most part, mainline denominations do not regularly include kinesthetic expressions in worship; we usually kneel, sit, or stand quietly to pray. About 20 percent of the population responds best to a kinesthetic modality, however, and individuals in this group often say that their most profound prayer occurs when they are running, swimming, cycling, or walking. Individuals who are aware of their kinesthetic predisposition can help reduce their stress by combining movement with their spiritual discipline.

Routes to Detachment

Sometimes after a stressful day, we arrive home and keep thinking about the things we could have managed better. Since stressful thoughts contribute to an increased stress level, it is important to find a route to detachment to take one's mind off work. Many people find that hobbies or activities unrelated to work keep them absorbed and help them relax.

Monitoring of Intake

As a generalization, North Americans are overfed but malnourished, consuming too much of the wrong kinds of food. They can improve their diet by careful monitoring of what they eat and drink. But monitoring of intake can also refer to controlling what movies or television they watch. Violence in either of those media jangles nerves and pollutes the psyche. It often takes many nights of dreaming to rid oneself of things taken in with the eyes and ears.

Regular Vigorous Exercise

We know that many of us have become couch potatoes. Our lack of vigorous exercise is one factor in the increasingly poor health of approximately 60 percent of our nation's population. Vigorous exercise on a regular basis can help reduce stress and contribute to good health. Many people find they exercise most faithfully if they do so at a specific time of day with a partner.

Assessing Your Stress

Below are two surveys that help in evaluating your level of stress and your response to it. Used together, the Clergy Life Changes Rating Scale, which indicates the amount of change a person has recently experienced, and the Strain Response Inventory, which measures physical symptoms related to stress, will help you understand how you are dealing with changes in your life. Strong scientific evidence indicates that the more social adjustments individuals make, the greater their chances of significant deterioration in health (Holmes and Rahe). Severe changes in health will themselves tend to increase the score even more.

Begin with the "Clergy Life Changes" Inventory. For each event that you believe you have experienced during the past 12 months, transfer the "Average Value" to the line in the "Your Score" column. The total is your overall Life Changes Score.

Then complete the Strain Response Inventory, following the instructions provided. The inventory measures whether you are living below, above, or just at your stress threshold. When individuals exceed their threshold level, physical symptoms of ill health may manifest themselves. The inventory identifies the physical symptoms that can occur.

Look at both scores to gauge the effects of change on you. Keep in mind that individuals vary in their tolerance for change, so the total Life Changes Score should be taken as a rough guide. Some people have enormous tolerance for chaos and flux and might score high on the life changes survey but show few physical symptoms of stress. A few people cannot tolerate even a few surprises in a day. For the most part, those with high scores also score high on the Strain Response Inventory. The key to interpreting your Life Changes Score, however, is the Strain Response Inventory.

In Closing

This article and the surveys can serve as a beginning for those who aim to reduce the impact of stress in their lives. It is important to note, however, that if serious stress continues, particularly when accompanied by an array of physical symptoms, counseling and possibly medical attention should be sought. A pastor who recognizes stress and works to reduce it, by whatever means, is demonstrating to congregants good stewardship of his or her body. Congregations need to make room for their pastors to engage in whatever stress-reducing activity seems to work for them. Both pastor and congregation will benefit from steps taken to become aware of stress and the work done to reduce it.

Notes

1. Kenneth R. Pelletier, *Mind as Healer, Mind as Slayer* (New York: Dell Publishing Co., 1977), p. 108.
2. John D. Adams, *Understanding and Managing Stress* (San Diego: University Associates Publishers, 1980), chap. 5.
3. Pelletier, *Mind as Healer,* p. 197.
4. Thomas Keating, *The Human Condition, Contemplation and Transformation* (New York: Paulist Press, 1999).
5. M. Basil Pennington, *Centering Prayer* (Garden City, N.Y.: Image Books, 1982).
6. Bio-Dots can be obtained inexpensively from Life Structure Resources, (800) 723-0625.
7. Roy M. Oswald, *How to Build a Support System for Your Ministry* (Bethesda, Md.: The Alban Institute, 1991; out of print). Discusses how forming clergy groups with competent leadership facilitates development of trust and a level of sharing that can lead to significant support.

Clergy Life Changes Rating Scale

Event	Average Value	Your Score
Death of spouse	100	
Divorce	73	
Marital separation	65	
Death of close family member	63	
Personal injury or illness	53	
Marriage	50	
Serious decline in church attendance	49	
Geographical relocation	49	
Private meetings by segment of congregation to discuss your resignation	47	
Beginning of heavy drinking by immediate family member	46	
Marital reconciliation	45	
Retirement	45	
Change in health of a family member	44	
Problem with children	42	
Pregnancy	40	
Sex difficulties	39	
Alienation from one's governing board	39	
Gain a new family member	39	
New job in new line of work	38	
Change in financial state	38	
Death of a close friend	37	
Increased arguing with spouse	35	
Merger of two or more congregations	35	
Troubled child in school	33	
Serious parish financial difficulty	32	
Mortgage over $150,000 for home	31	
Difficulty with member of church staff (associates, organist, choir director, secretary, janitor, etc.)	31	

CLERGY EXPERIENCING TRANSITION

Event	Average Value	Your Score
Difficulty finding adequate child care	30	
Destruction of church by fire	30	
New job same line of work	30	
Son or daughter leaving home	29	
Trouble with in-laws	29	
Anger of influential church member over pastor action	29	
Slow steady decline in church attendance	29	
Outstanding personal achievement	29	
Introduction of new hymnal to worship service	28	
Failure of the church to make payroll	27	
Remodeling or building program	27	
Start or stop of spouse's employment	26	
Holiday away	26	
Start or finish of school	26	
Death of peer	26	
Offer of call to another congregation	26	
Change in living conditions	25	
Revision of personal habits	24	
Negative congregational activity by former pastor	24	
Difficulty with confirmation class	22	
Change in residence	20	
Change in schools	20	
Change in recreation	19	
Change in social activities	18	
Death or moving away of good church leader	18	
Mortgage or personal loan of less than $150,000	17	
Change in sleeping habits	16	
Development of new friendships	16	
Change in eating habits	15	
Stressful continuing education experience	15	
Major program change	15	
Vacation at home	13	
Christmas	12	
Lent	12	
Easter	12	
Minor violation of the law	11	
YOUR TOTAL		

This Life Changes Rating Scale was adapted by Roy M. Oswald from the Holmes/Rahe Scale and field-tested with clergy groups from various denominations. See T. H. Homes and R. H. Rahe, "The Social Readjustment Rating Scale," *Journal of Psychosomatic Research,* vol. 2 (1967): 213–218.

STRAIN RESPONSE INVENTORY

Use numbers to indicate how often you experience each behavior on the list.

0 = Never
1 = Infrequently
2 = Frequently
3 = Regularly

_____ 1. Eat too much
_____ 2. Drink too much alcohol
_____ 3. Smoke more than usual
_____ 4. Feel tense, uptight, and fidgety
_____ 5. Feel depressed or remorseful
_____ 6. Like myself less
_____ 7. Have difficulty going to sleep or staying asleep
_____ 8. Feel restless and unable to concentrate
_____ 9. Have decreased interest in sex
_____ 10. Have increased interest in sex
_____ 11. Have loss of appetite
_____ 12. Feel tired/low energy
_____ 13. Feel irritable
_____ 14. Think about suicide
_____ 15. Become less communicative
_____ 16. Feel disoriented or overwhelmed

_____ 17. Have difficulty getting up in the morning
_____ 18. Have headaches
_____ 19. Have upset stomach
_____ 20. Have sweaty and/or trembling hands
_____ 21. Have shortness of breath and sighing
_____ 22. Let things slide
_____ 23. Misdirect anger
_____ 24. Feel "unhealthy"
_____ 25. Feel time bound, anxious about too much to do in too little time
_____ 26. Use prescription drugs to relax
_____ 27. Use medication for high blood pressure
_____ 28. Depend on recreational drugs to relax
_____ 29. Have anxiety about the future
_____ 30. Have back problems
_____ 31. Unable to clear up a cold, running nose, sore throat, cough, infection, etc.
_____ TOTAL SCORE (Add up all your numbers)

Interpreting Your Score

0 to 20 Below average strain in your life.

21 to 30 Stress starting to show its effects in your life. You are living life near your stress threshold and at times crossing it.

31 to 40 Above average strain. Stress is having a very destructive effect on your life. You are living a good portion of your life beyond your stress threshold.

40 and higher Unless you do something soon to alleviate your stress, more serious illness will follow.

Note

Adapted from "The Strain Response" by John D. Adams and used with permission of the author.

CT 3

TRANSITIONS FOR CLERGY SPOUSES

A MOVE FROM ONE LOCATION TO ANOTHER always produces stress, because it requires adjustments to every detail of life in a new community. Alban Institute seminars for clergy and spouses have revealed that it may be more difficult for the pastor's spouse than for the pastor to make a transition from one congregation to another. In stress surveys administered to both, the indications of stress were almost always higher for spouses than for the clergy. Sessions with spouses alone uncovered some of the reasons for this. This article addresses some of the difficulties that clergy spouses experience, and offers suggestions for ways to alleviate the stress that results.

Role Expectations

Clergy spouses, especially wives, are not always viewed simply as members of the congregation. While other members of the congregation are free to choose the activities in which they will participate, there is often an unstated expectation that the pastor's spouse should be prominently involved in many activities; this may be the case especially when the former pastor's spouse was immersed in congregational life. It is important for both pastor and spouse to assert firmly but pleasantly that the spouse is an individual member of the

congregation in the spouse's own right, and not some kind of unpaid assistant to the pastor.

Lack of Pastoral Care

Who is the pastor to the pastor's spouse? Often no one provides this care. A clergy spouse who is experiencing personal problems, particularly at home or spiritually, cannot seek counsel from the clergy member, who may even be part of the problem. And if the spouse's concern is something about the pastor, it may seem difficult to confide in someone without fear of jeopardizing the pastor's career.

It is important that the spouse not feel obliged to bear such problems alone. It is appropriate for a clergy spouse to seek out another clergyperson in the community, possibly someone who has become known through clergy family networking, though it might be better to avoid someone with whom pastor and spouse socialize together. Finding a spiritual director or spiritual friend may provide the needed support; Roman Catholic brothers and sisters and, increasingly, Protestant clergy and laity trained for that ministry may be available in the area. In some cases, clergy spouses may choose to become members of another congregation. If this becomes a topic of concern for members who feel implied criticism of the congregation, the intervention of the pastor/parish relations committee may be useful (see CT 4); the committee should remind congregants that the spouse does not come as part of a package with the pastor. If professional counseling becomes necessary, the spouse should seek out a qualified counselor in the community.

Lack of Support

While the pastor can fit into the new role quickly and has many opportunities to develop relationships in both congregation and community, the spouse who does not work outside the home may find developing relationships more difficult. Friendships take time to develop and spouses may feel guarded in contacts with members of the congregation, to whom they do not want to reveal family problems. Developing a support system takes time and work, but the clergy spouse should seek opportunities to affirm her or his own individuality and interests. When there are children in the family, contacts with other families with children of the same age make it easier to form relationships in the community. A spouse can seek out organizations or activities in the community that draw people with similar interests; these have the additional advantage of being outside of the realm of the congregation. In addition, newcomer organizations in many communities provide a structure for meeting people who are also experiencing transitions. Clergy-spouse peer groups are generally not successful, as they tend to draw people back into the realm of church-related concerns.

Living in Congregation-Provided Housing

Clergy sometimes have little choice about their housing: the congregation owns a house and expects the pastor to live in it. The best way to minimize problems in this area is for the pastor to fully negotiate housing arrangements as part of the letter of agreement, as described in PT 19. Many problems related to housing can be avoided by an understanding, before the family moves in, that the church-owned house is the pastor's home, and that it should be respected as is the home of any other person in the congregation. It is usually clergy spouses, however, who feel the most pressure when the home is not kept immaculately clean.

Finances and Working Spouses

No one gets rich on a clergy salary, and many clergy couples feel the financial pinch. Many clergy spouses are members of the workforce, for their own satisfaction and to supplement family income. If a spouse works 9 to 5 on weekdays and the pastor has to work evenings and weekends, it will be difficult for them to find time together. The couple will need to make a conscious effort to arrange their schedule so that they will have time with each other and their family. The pastor might decide to use the weekday "day off" to do personal errands and chores, so that Saturday could be a family day. The pastor might also ask that evening meetings not begin immediately after the dinner hour, allowing early evening time with the family.

Being Disenfranchised

Clergy spouses often feel like second-class citizens in a congregation. Congregants hope that the pastor's spouse will be an active, involved, and friendly member of the congregation, but often expect that the spouse will never take a stand on a congregational issue or run for a congregation office. There is no easy solution to this dilemma other than for the spouse to be involved patiently yet determinedly with the group or groups that appeal to the spouse's tastes and talents, building a reputation as a trusted and reliable participant, but not one who seeks a role in the governance of the congregation.

The Strain on Clergy Marriages

Congregational ministry can be hard on marriages. The demands of time, sympathetic dealing with the problems of others, and life in a "fishbowl" atmosphere (particularly in family- and pastoral-size congregations) can take their toll. It is easy for a clergy couple to take their marriage for granted, and to assume that because one of them does marriage counseling, they might not need help themselves. Good marriages require hard work, and this is especially true for a clergy marriage. A strong case can be made for clergy and their spouses to participate in marriage enrichment seminars, and even to use continuing education funds to pay for them. These seminars provide tools for monitoring a marriage relationship and keeping it healthy; they can provide a context in which to review the quality of their life together and to make joint decisions that will improve the relationship. Marriage enrichment seminars are for good marriages, and part of the clergy couple's ministry to the congregation can be to model the process of assessing and strengthening a good marriage.

Conclusion

A pastor's spouse is likely to have some idea of what marriage to a member of the clergy will be like: it will involve adaptation to a very special life in which the job is basically full time. A move of the clergyperson to a new congregation creates many sources of tension, but it can also offer a spouse the opportunity to create a role and lifestyle of their own, and even enhance the marriage relationship. Both spouses should be aware of their need for support to keep their marriage healthy. They should, therefore, make an effort when moving into a new community to seek friends outside the congregation who can support them and help keep their relationship strong.

CT 4

FORMING A PASTOR/PARISH RELATIONS COMMITTEE

MOST MEMBERS OF A CONGREGATION see the pastor only once a week at Sunday services; they do not see the many forms of ministry to individuals or small groups that take place during the week, and may be unaware of the pastor's other unseen activities on behalf of the congregation. Members expect the pastor to conduct worship services and be present with congregation members in crisis, but are not sure what else the pastor needs to do. The pastor can be spending 70-hour weeks on the job and still not feel that everything has been done. At the same time, some members of the congregation may be wondering, "What does the pastor do with all that free time?" It is easy for a pastor to feel overwhelmed and underappreciated. Resentment can build up and destroy the pastor's self-confidence and devotion to the congregation. What can be done when pastor and congregation are moving toward misunderstandings such as these?

The Pastor/Parish Relations Committee

The pastor needs help, and a pastor/parish relations committee (PPRC) can provide at least some of it. A PPRC provides understanding and support to the pastor by learning about the unique demands their congregation places on its clergy and about the

expectations the pastor has of the congregation. It monitors the relationship between the pastor and congregation, and makes recommendations to both the pastor and the board to suggest things that will help keep that relationship positive and mutually supportive. Thus it fosters an atmosphere that allows the congregation to grow and flourish in exciting ways. Because this committee is of primary benefit to the pastor, the pastor has a significant role in the selection of its members, the setting of agendas, and in the formation of recommendations it makes.[1]

Structuring the Pastor/Parish Relations Committee

Some important things to consider when forming the PPRC are committee size, method of selecting members, frequency and nature of meetings, preservation of confidentiality, and relationship to the governing board.

Membership

A committee of four to six is large enough to offer a variety of perspectives and feedback to the pastor but small enough to become a close and trusting group. In some congregations, the pastor nominates a larger group from which the board makes selections, though it may be difficult for a new pastor to suggest names especially when the pastor does not know members of the congregation very well. In some cases, pastors have chosen members of the search committee with whom they worked particularly well; sometimes pastors will use the previous pastor's committee for the first year or so. Members must command the trust of both congregation and pastor, and the board must have confidence in this committee, since it will be asked to take the PPRC's advice seriously. Since it takes time for both trust and an appreciation of the pastor's position to develop, members of the committee should serve for more than a year, and their terms should overlap so that there is always continuity from one year to the next.

Meetings

The pastor and committee need to meet often enough to develop an open and supportive relationship. During the first few months, the pastor may want to meet every couple of weeks to get help tracking the unfolding relationship with the congregation. Meeting with this frequency will also help speed the development of the trusting relationship between pastor and committee members. After this initial period, monthly meetings should be sufficient; as the pastor's tenure lengthens, pastor and committee may decide that less frequent meetings are needed.

Meetings of the committee may be loosely structured to foster communication, the frank expression of concerns, and a free-flowing consideration of what to do about them. For the first few months, committee members need to learn about what the position of pastor requires in terms of activities and time. The committee might ask the pastor to log for a couple of weeks how much time is spent in a variety of areas: visitation (crisis, noncrisis, hospital), committee meetings, administrative functions, sermon and worship preparation, study, spiritual development, and so forth.

If the pastor is coming to feel that there is not enough time to do everything the position requires, the committee can help examine what activities might be delegated or even left unattended. If the pastor feels that a particular area of congregational life needs more attention from the pastor, the committee may have suggestions about how members might pick up the slack in other areas.

The PPRC can also introduce matters of interest or concern from the congregation's perspective; for example, if the committee is aware that the pastor's actions are, in some way, alienating some members of the congregation, the concern can be raised and the committee can work with the pastor to see how the situation can be addressed before it becomes a major problem. In such cases, the mere voicing of a concern can be enough to initiate a productive discussion in which both pastor and committee learn something important about themselves and one another.

Confidentiality

This committee can accomplish its goals only when pastor and lay members are completely open and honest with one another. For this to happen, the pastor must be certain that matters which the PPRC discusses will be kept absolutely confidential and never talked about outside committee meetings. Likewise, members of the committee must be certain that neither pastor nor other committee members will pass on to others anything they have said. Trust in one another will develop as time passes and as everyone sees that confidentiality has been maintained. (The suggestions in PT 11 relating to confidentiality may be useful for this committee.)

Relationship to the Governing Board

Since meetings of the PPRC are confidential, no formal minutes should be kept. The committee should report that it has met, but not give details of the topics of discussion, unless the committee has specific recommendations for the board to which the committee members and pastor agree.

What the Pastor/Parish Relations Committee Is Not

Because the PPRC is formed to support the pastor, there are a number of things this committee can never do. It cannot conduct evaluations or salary reviews of the pastor, and should not serve as a personnel committee. In addition, the PPRC must remember that it is not a decision-making body; any recommendations regarding the congregation's relationship with the pastor are referred to the board for action. Finally, committee members must resist the temptation to be channels to the pastor for individuals' complaints; in most cases, individuals can and should address their personal concerns to the pastor directly. To be sure, there will be occasions when individuals or groups are so upset that the committee will need to discuss the cause of this concern for the sake of the congregation and to try to rebuild the personal relationships that

may be fragmenting. In such a case it is essential that the committee raise the issue, hear what the pastor has to say about it, and then discuss how to address it. The PPRC may discuss how serious the situation actually is, examine possible responses to it, or ask its members or the pastor or both to address an individual's issues face to face to work toward a solution.

The Success of the Pastor/Parish Relations Committee

The true test of the committee's effectiveness comes when concerns are handled in a way that leaves both pastor and lay members confident that they have worked well together and found a solution that will benefit the congregation. The congregation is likely to be unaware of the workings of the committee, but if it does its work well, the congregation will realize the benefits of the process. They will be freed, in large measure, from conflict and dissatisfaction and will be ready to join the pastor in satisfying and exciting expressions of worship and witness.

Note

1. A videotape that examines the formation of a PPRC is Roy M. Oswald, *Why You Should Develop a Pastor-Parish Relations Committee* (Bethesda, Md.: The Alban Institute, 2001).

CT 5

Discovering the Psychological Contracts of Members

As people develop relationships, they form unspoken, nonrational, and often unconscious expectations of each other. Individuals within the relationship have a strong sense and expectation of "how things should be." For the most part, individuals in these relationships perform as expected; they may become worried or upset when others act in ways that are unexpected or feel inappropriate. Such expectations develop in part because of the history that the people in the relationship share; but individual expectations sometimes develop because of a person's past experiences in other relationships. This sense of how things should be can be described as a "psychological contract": *psychological*, because it originates and is evaluated (even if unconsciously) in the minds of the participants, and *contract*, because there is an agreement (even if unspoken) that things will happen in a certain way.

For example, two professional friends may develop the habit of having lunch on a monthly basis, always rescheduling if one has to cancel. They always go to the same restaurant, each paying their own way, and talk almost exclusively about business. The friend who reads broadly may bring an article or book for the other, though the other would never reciprocate. These friends would never expect to visit one another at home; it would not occur to them to make a foursome with their spouses, or even to include another professional in their lunch. The details of this routine have probably never been discussed, but if you asked each member of the pair to describe the psychological contract between them, their descriptions would be close.

Psychological contracts also develop within groups of people. Consider a prayer group that always meets at 7 P.M. on Mondays at Ellen's house. Originally her house was the most central; it no longer is so, but the group still meets there. They start only when Tom arrives; he is usually a bit late, because of his work and a tendency to procrastinate. No refreshments are served, but there is always a pitcher of ice water and tray of glasses on the table. Lucy always leads off and Hal always remembers the homeless shelter. George makes announcements about the group at worship services. While this group's practices have developed without explicit agreement for the most part, changes are not made without discussion. Though the group says its membership is open, some newcomers may feel uncomfortable or even unwelcome; some people will work into the group and eventually find their particular role, while others may simply decide that the group is "not for them." Newcomers who stay are comfortable with the psychological contract the group members have developed, while those who move on are not.

Psychological contracts are also made in congregations. Every member has a contract with both congregation and pastor. They do certain things for the congregation (weed the garden, sing in the choir, or just attend worship) but not others (don't ask *me* to teach church school); they also expect certain things in return from both congregation and pastor. The contracts members have with the pastor often differ by congregation size. In a family-size congregation, members have long-established contracts with one another rather than with the pastor. In a pastoral-size congregation, members often expect a personal relationship with the pastor. In program-size congregations, the pastor will have a relationship with people who run programs, as well as the power people in the congregation. Other members may not expect a personal relationship with the pastor, but they do expect that she will see that events happen on schedule, and might expect a good sermon every week. In corporate-size congregations, the senior pastor will have different kinds of contracts with staff members, power people, and other members of the congregation. The complexity of the different contracts will vary according to the degree of interaction the pastor has with individuals.

When members are upset with either the congregation or the pastor, it is usually because the unspoken, often unconscious psychological contract has been broken. This creates a particular challenge for a new pastor, who may have inherited the contracts that members had with the predecessor. Clergy should realize that much of this contract will surface in their first substantial meeting with a member; role negotiation of the contract may be going on at the first meeting, whether it is conscious or not.

For example, on a first visit with one member, the pastor may hear in effect, "Pastor, I will be in church on Christmas and Easter, and maybe a few times in between,

but don't expect a whole lot more from me. Please don't ask me to serve on any committee or even be an usher. Please bury me when I die, and give some attention to my wife if she is ill or distressed." On the first visit with another member, the pastor may learn that this person will be in church every Sunday and wants to serve on several committees. It may emerge that this person has had ready access to the pastor when problems arise, and enjoys being the pastor's confidante.

Clearly, these people want different relationships with both congregation and pastor, and the pastor will interact with them differently. It is important to recognize that certain factors may have been part of a person's psychological contract with the former pastor, and this member could be offended when the new pastor "breaks the contract." The wise new pastor will listen for clues to the psychological contract members have with the congregation as a whole, as well as the contract they had with the former pastor. The pastor may find it better to ask specific questions about members' relationships with the congregation and the former pastor at early meetings in order to learn what relationship they expect. It may be helpful for the pastor to make a card file, and take a few minutes *in private* after each conversation to write down perceptions of the contracts that various members have and want with congregation and pastor. It is important to remember that any note taking must not be visible to members of the congregation, lest they feel the pastor is spying on them. The notes are important because they help the new pastor see quickly if the right questions have been asked in order to reveal a clear sense of a congregant's psychological contract. Developing the skill of asking the right questions will make the pastor's visits more purposeful, in addition to merely building relationships with members.

Perhaps the pastor will need to renegotiate the pastoral role with certain members. For example, a pastor visiting a homebound member may learn that she expects a pastoral call once a month. The pastor might respond by saying, "Mabel, I usually call on people once a quarter. Can you accept me as your pastor if that is the case?" If Mabel says no, considerable tension will exist unless the pastor can find an alternative way to meet Mabel's needs (e.g., by establishing a lay calling committee, or touching base with an occasional phone call) or unless Mabel accepts the new pastor's way of ministering to her. If the differences between Mabel's expectations and the pastor's style of ministry are not resolved, their relationship may always be strained.

Gaining information about different members' psychological contracts will help the pastor become a better spiritual guide to each one. It will help the pastor identify the type of relationship that each member expects, negotiate a set of expectations that both can accept, and help empower members to perform the ministries to which they are called.

THE "HONEYMOON PERIOD" OF A NEW PASTORATE

THE OPENING MONTHS of a new pastorate, when everything seems to be going extremely well, are often referred to as a "honeymoon period." At least this is how it seems to the new pastor. The members of the congregation appear to appreciate, listen to, and respect their new pastor. But just when the pastor is inclined to say that the start-up period is successful, the impression changes. The pastor becomes aware that some people are not happy, even criticizing the pastor's actions. People seem to be judging the whole search process and its result more negatively. What is going on?

This phenomenon occurs in enough new pastorates to be worth examining. The mere perception that the situation has changed for the worse can affect the pastor's self-esteem and confident handling of the congregation. Is it something the pastor has caused? Are the critics right, and has the pastor's ministry not been what the congregation really wanted and needed? Or is the phenomenon just a natural, if unsettling, feature of a group experiencing new leadership? Although it is likely that the last explanation best describes the situation, it is still necessary to find out if some cause for concern exists. An awareness of the dynamics of the honeymoon period can relieve a pastor's anxiety by suggesting that its end is a natural phenomenon and can also direct the pastor's attention to signs of matters of real concern.

This article summarizes the features of three theories of the honeymoon period in the early stages of a new pastorate. Since the effects of the ending of this period can last well beyond the first year, those interested in a discussion of the later stages of the phenomenon, as well as full details on the early stages, are referred to the sources of these theories. All three theories argue that ultimately a healthy and accurately perceived relationship between pastor and congregation develops after the honeymoon illusions have been dispersed.

Community Formation and the Honeymoon Period

M. Scott Peck[1] describes the honeymoon period as the first of four stages a group goes through as it seeks to form community: pseudo-community, chaos, emptiness, and community. In pseudo-community, people are "nice" to one another, wanting things to develop well, not voicing any discontent or disillusionment. Whether this niceness represents a genuine feeling or a pose adopted to avoid hurting others' feelings, nothing has challenged it yet.

But then the second phase, chaos, breaks out in an expression of bad feelings that results in conflict. One cause of this conflict may be that people have differing views on the real basis of the community, with little agreement on its norms and standards. If that is indeed the case, this phase can last a long time, a year or much more. The group escapes the conflict only by entering the phase of emptiness, in which people surrender their individual views of what constitutes the ideal community. From this emptiness a true community emerges through an appreciation of the views of individual members and the uniqueness of the shared community they constitute.

In terms of a pastoral transition, the arrival of a new pastor creates a pseudo-community in a congregation whose identity is inextricably bound up with the relationship of its members to the pastor. Chaos begins when some congregants begin to feel the wrong person was chosen as pastor, and conflict within the congregation and between congregants and pastor ensues. A resolution is only reached as the congregation comes to terms with one another and with the pastor.

The Honeymoon Period as a "Crisis of Authentication"

John Fletcher[2] identifies three "crises (or phases) of authentication" that clergy must go through successively before they are accepted as effective spiritual leaders of a congregation: these phases are personal, professional, and particular authenticity. The first crisis is preceded by a phase (the honeymoon) in which congregations try, in subtle or not so subtle ways, to get to know the pastor better; that is, find out if the image of caring and competence the pastor projects conforms to the reality (although some congregations never engage in this testing and thus remain in a superficial relationship).

The subtle testing through which members seek a deeper relationship with the pastor (and in which the congregation may also be testing its own authenticity) develops into a period of anxiety for pastor and

congregation, each eager to please self and other but afraid of being found wanting in some way. A pattern of avoidance of self-discovery can lead to a dull routine, an acceptance of a static status quo. An attempt to transcend the stasis and to move to a healthier, vital relationship (for example, by the pastor's proposing a new program or a change in an existing one) can lead to a conflict through the exposure of people's real feelings. This ending of the honeymoon corresponds to Peck's chaos phase.

When the first conflict ends with the pastor perceived as passing the congregation's testing, the pastor achieves Fletcher's second phase, professional authenticity. But the pastor ultimately faces a second crisis, as a result of feeling uncomfortable with or unable to live up to the new image of competence the first crisis gave rise to. The congregation can resolve this crisis by coming to the pastor's aid and showing that the congregation can compensate for certain weaknesses of the pastor. In the resulting phase of particular authenticity, the pastor recognizes the need to focus on those aspects of ministry for which the pastor's talents are best suited and to share responsibility for these and other areas with the congregation.

The Honeymoon as Romanticizing the Pastor

Warner White[3] describes three phases of the way a pastor and congregation come to know each other: the romance of magnification, the loss of illusions, and the pedestal problem. The first phase refers to the tendency of congregants to romanticize their new pastor; that is, to idealize or "magnify" the pastor's qualities (again, phenomena typical of the honeymoon period). White sees congregants as transferring their spiritual longings to the new pastor; that is, they see the pastor as a person in whom they can invest their deepest hopes and desires. (White also notes that a kind of negative magnification can also occur when a congregation transfers to a new pastor the feelings of a betrayal that an earlier pastor brought on by failing to live up to the members' expectations.) Clergy, too, can romanticize their congregation, seeing them as, for example, idealized participants in adult education classes or as model missioners to the poor.

White claims that some congregations remain stuck in this romanticizing phase (the honeymoon), just as Fletcher observes that some remain in the first phase of authenticity, and so never really come to know their pastor or vice-versa. Successful congregations and pastors, however, go through a phase of losing illusions about their own qualities and those of the other party. This disillusionment can have two results. Exceptionally, pastor and congregation can turn negative and magnify the other's faults instead of virtues, a real crisis for the relationship between pastor and congregation. Normally, however, the congregation and pastor decide to accept themselves and each other with all their faults and limitations, as well as their real virtues, and build a relationship on the basis of this acceptance. This solution is based on a resolution of what can also be called the "pedestal problem." Both pastor and congregation

fall off the metaphorical pedestal they have created for themselves and each other; but in doing so, they discover real strengths on which a productive relationship can be based.

Conclusion

These theories are similar in the ways they characterize the dynamics of a group's reactions to a change in an essential component of its identity: in the case of a congregation, the arrival of a new pastor. The first tendency of the group is to paper over any sense of disappointment; but after that, the natural reaction is to express the bottled up feelings of disillusionment. This expression has the potential to destroy the group's identity, but much more commonly it functions as the impetus necessary to draw the group into a form of community that much more truly reflects its nature and purposes.

A new pastor (and the congregation the pastor serves) should take heart from these findings and realize, when the first major crisis in a pastorate occurs, that it is an opportunity for the congregation and pastor to bring an uncertain relationship into one that more truly reflects the potential of both pastor and congregation.

Notes

1. M. Scott Peck, *The Different Drum: Community Making and Peace* (New York: Touchstone, 1987).

2. John Fletcher, *Religious Authenticity in the Clergy* (Washington, D.C.: The Alban Institute, 1985).

3. Warner White, "Eager Longing: Developing Reverence for One Another," *Congregations*, November/December 1998.

CT 7

PREPARING TO MAKE CHANGES

THE BIGGEST CHALLENGE for a new pastor is to control the desire to make changes during the first few months. Thirty years as a church consultant have convinced Roy Oswald that before making any changes in a congregation, a new pastor should first identify the most important changes needed to move the congregation to greater health and growth. Almost everyone will say yes to a new pastor at least once; that moment of agreement should be saved for something that is really important to the congregation.

Many clergy in new pastorates rush to make cosmetic changes, rather than changes with real substance. Most often, these changes are in the corporate worship of the congregation—probably the worst place to make changes, since they affect the greatest number of people most quickly and in the least rational feature of congregational life. A pastor who begins to use a modern version of the Lord's Prayer when the congregation is used to the traditional version, or introduces a new kind of music upsets many people in the congregation, uses up the tolerance for change that many of them have, and changes nothing of substance.

In the 1970s, several research projects in which Oswald participated focused on U.S. Army chaplains in new assignments. Supervising chaplains were asked what

seemed to get the younger ones in trouble fastest in a new assignment. Almost always, the answer was that they arrived at a new assignment with a congregational program in the hip pocket. These chaplains were ready to "do their thing" before they got to know members of the congregation and learn whether their favorite program was really needed. They were flying blind, saying to the congregation, "I don't care who you are or what you might want; I know this is right for you."

When a pastor makes changes before getting to know the congregation, people feel that the pastor is rejecting not only their way of worshiping God and their programs, but also them personally. With the feeling of rejection comes the thought, "If you really love us, why did you come in and change our way of doing things?" Rather, a new pastor should spend the first 9 to 12 months being a lover and a historian.

Become a Lover

The lover finds something to love in everyone. Clergy probably underestimate how important it is for people to sense that their pastor likes them. Clergy tend to be more anxious about whether or not people think they are competent and so devote their energy to trying to demonstrate competence.

While competence is important, it is less so than loving people. It certainly makes a difference to people to feel that the pastor is glad to see them week after week.

In some clergy start-up seminars, Oswald sends clergy to a shopping mall to sit and watch people for a couple of hours. As people walk by, the clergy are to lock in on one person at a time and ask themselves, "Would I like to have that person in my congregation?" When they do this, they realize that they are attracted to certain people and turned off by others on the basis of physical appearance alone, and thus become more aware of how easily likes and dislikes can be formed. They learn that they must work hard at being a caring pastor to some members of the congregation. A new pastor who spends time with individuals is likely to find something that is admirable in each of them, and by focusing on their admirable traits can make a special connection with each one. Being a lover for 9 to 12 months, getting to know people well enough to find the things about them that are likeable, actually pays off.

Size of congregation determines those with whom clergy need to work hardest at finding something to love. In a family-size congregation (Sunday attendance of 50 or fewer), the pastor usually has little influence with the "patriarchs" and "matriarchs." In such a congregation, the pastor will of necessity come to know all members and should try to develop the role of lover with each of them. In a pastoral-size congregation (Sunday attendance of 50 to 150), much of the spiritual development of people comes through the relationship they have with their pastor. In such a congregation, the new pastor should try to visit every member in their home at least once during the first 9 to 12 months, and work to find something to love in each of them. After that, any proposed changes in congregation life are much more likely to be received with openness and trust. In a program-size congregation (attendance of 150 to 350), the new pastor should de-velop the role of lover with the core leaders of the congregation, the people who run the programs that meet people's spiritual needs. Building rapport with the movers and shakers of the congregation will win their support when the first major change is proposed. In a corporate-size congregation (attendance of 350 and higher), the role of lover relates to members of the parish staff and to the power people in the congregation, without whose endorsement changes in programs or mission outreach might falter.

It takes a new pastor 9 to 12 months to establish the kind of "liking" relationship with the congregants who influence decisions to pave the way for any major change the pastor may propose, especially a controversial one. A pastor who plans a significant change at this point should learn the thoughts and feelings of the leaders before going out on a limb for it. If signs of opposition appear, the pastor can take steps to overcome it or modify the proposal. The article on "power analysis" of a congregation (see CT 8) suggests a way for clergy to gauge their power and authority within a congregation by rating their relationship with the power people in the congregation. But a pastor can accomplish more by being perceived as a lover than as only an authority figure.

The effect of being loved by the pastor has other results. Over time, clergy unconsciously rearrange the involvement people have with their congregation by favoring the people they like and seeing that those people get to serve on important committees. Clergy tend to overlook people they do not like in recommending committee leaders, because they find themselves disagreeing with them on a personal level even when their perspective on an issue is right on. The article on leadership shifts after a pastoral transition (see ET 3) shows that while about 20 percent of the membership provides 80 percent of both the leadership and financial support in almost every congregation, the leadership group tends to change after a new pastor arrives; to a core of people the new pastor likes.

Become a Historian

In addition to being a lover for the first 9 to 12 months in a new congregation, the pastor should become a historian of the congregation. An easy way for the pastor to do this is by attending a historical reflection event (see PT 21). By learning the history of the congregation, the new pastor can begin to see more clearly how and why the congregation functions as a total system, and why some of its preferences and practices have become so firmly established. An understanding of the congregation's history may help the pastor decide which changes can be made, and on what time schedule. If the congregation does not propose a historical reflection event, the wise and caring pastor might ask the board to arrange one, describing what it involves, and how it will help the pastor get to know the congregation better.

Making Changes

The first change a new pastor introduces should be a major one, which, if successful, will move the congregation to a new level of living and loving. It should ready the congregation for significant growth in numbers by increasing and enhancing its spiritual depth, social outreach, and care for its members. When a congregation grows in these three areas of congregational life, numbers are likely to grow too.

Postponing this change for the first 9 to 12 months has several advantages. First, the pastor has had time to establish good relationships. Congregation members who feel that their pastor knows and cares about them are much more likely to follow the pastor's lead. Second, the pastor has had time to identify and establish a working relationship with the influential members of the congregation. The pastor has found out where the land mines are and can avoid them when proceeding with the change. Third, and most important, the pastor has come to know the key issues facing the congregation, and can identify the change that will best promote the congregation's health. A pastor who has gotten to know the congregation in this gradual, purposeful way will not attempt to implement a "one size fits all" programmatic change, but rather one directly related to this particular congregation.

Hence the importance of not making changes too early. The only secure way to make change is by understanding the congregation and securing the trust of those with the most influence in decision-making, and persuading them that a particular change is necessary. While there are cases in which an early change has succeeded, that is not usually the case. Early changes are risky and many pastors who have tried early changes that failed miserably have doomed their ministry in the congregation ever after. Of course, with every rule there are exceptions. The challenge for clergy beginning a new pastorate is to decide if some unique circumstances require immediate attention. In any case, any change a pastor and congregation decide upon, at whatever point in their life together, should be based on broad support and prayerful consideration.

CT 8

POWER ANALYSIS OF A CONGREGATION

WE CANNOT ESCAPE the fact that a congregation is also a political community. Every community of three or more is in some sense a political entity. Someone will need to lead, and others will need to follow, even though the leader/follower roles may shift from member to member at different times. Power and authority issues are particularly relevant when all the followers cannot obtain everything they want in a particular decision and some compromise needs to be struck. Congregational leaders at this point may be tempted to avoid facing the conflict between members' needs and wants, refusing to lead until it is "safe" to do so. What is required, however, is for parish leaders to offer the leadership necessary to help members face their differences, which requires that leaders come to terms with power and authority issues.

My Own Personal Journey with Power

I [Roy] wish I had understood all this when I began professional ministry some 40 years ago. I believed then that correct ideas and a good heart could change a church overnight into a dynamic, growing organism. After I had waded into a few parish skirmishes and gotten blown out of the water by some astute lay people, I realized that I was missing skills as a change agent.

I was not, however, without power in those early years of ministry. The minute I arrived on the scene with the label "pastor," authority was granted to me. The weight of this authority frightened me at first. I was often confused by the fact that I carried so much authority in some respects, yet was powerless to effect changes I thought were important for the parish. With time, and with the support of many dedicated lay people who came to my aid, I was able to get a good number of things accomplished. For the most part, however, I was ignorant of the power dynamics in the congregation. Although I made many power moves and observed other individuals and groups moving with power and force, I did not have a cognitive map of where I was going or understand that I needed power to get there. I had little insight into others' need to act with power to sustain their investment in the parish. I did not sense the need to empower the alienated members of the congregation. I had no strategy for empowering the solid congregational members who could not communicate well.

After continuing to stub my toe on power and authority issues for several years, I became involved in human relations training. I began to gain insight into power issues through the Mid-Atlantic Association for Training and Consulting (MATC). They asked me to coordinate a lab in power and conflict with the help of a consultant, George Peabody of Peabody Associates, who worked with me for two years and encouraged me to go to a two-month symposium on power sponsored by the Industrial Area Foundation (Saul D. Alinsky Institute). It was there that I learned about how power relates to community formation and action.

To come to grips with power, I first needed to come to terms with my self-interest and the self-interest of others. Self-interest is the prime mover of people. It motivates all of us. I had to learn to distinguish between self-interest and selfishness or self-centeredness. Hans Selye, in his book, *Stress Without Distress*, is clear on this issue:

> Egotism or selfishness is the most ancient characteristic feature of life. From the simplest microorganism to man, all living beings must protect their own interests first of all. . . . Curiously, despite our inborn egotism, many of us are strongly motivated by altruistic feelings. Yet, these two apparently contradictory impulses are not incompatible; the instinct for self-preservation need not conflict with the wish to help others. Altruism can be regarded as a modified form of egotism, a kind of collective selfishness that helps the community in that it engenders gratitude. . . . I believe that the potentially explosive and dangerous, but inevitable, drive of egotism has been gradually defused by a marriage with altruism and that the resulting altruistic egotism can lead to mutually satisfactory peaceful cooperation between competitive cells, organs, people, and even entire societies."[1]

If I am a pastor of a congregation, it is not in my self-interest for certain members of the congregation to feel powerless and unheard when decisions affect them. I need to be clear about and aware of my self-interest as I work with issues and people, a

difficult challenge especially when I am caught up in emotionally laden situations. I also need to come to grips with my theology of power. I used to think using power meant coercing or manipulating people and that ultimately power corrupts. But I have come to believe that God gives us power and wants us to be powerful. All of us are called to be effective in unique ways, and in order to be effective, we need to be powerful. If power is the ability to get something done, then we all need lots of power because there is a lot God wants us to do, and I need to risk using as much power as my particular calling requires.

Clergy new to their congregations may have a "grace" period of nine to twelve months, but eventually the congregation is going to want them to assume leadership to do God's calling—to ensure that the congregation will be vibrant, healthy, and growing. In order to do that, clergy have to work with the power people within the congregation. It would be prudent for them, therefore, to get to know these people, find out what their self-interests are within the congregation, and begin building relationships of trust and respect in order to gain support for important changes in the congregation.

This article will help church leaders understand more clearly the power dynamics within their congregations. It offers a tool for analyzing various power currencies available within congregations and for learning how to use those currencies to reach positive goals. And it will help church leaders come to grips with their theology of power and in the process to become more comfortable using the power and authority available to them. We begin with an overall look at the phenomenon of power.

Power Is Not a Dirty Word

Power is the ability to get what you want. Whenever you are able to do that—whether you hang new curtains in the church kitchen or persuade a congregation to sponsor a 10-story facility for seniors—

you are a powerful person in that congregation. Power is the ability to mobilize resources to be used effectively to reach specific ends. In and of itself, power is neither good nor evil. It can become good or evil, however, depending on what ends it is used to reach and the means used to attain those desired goals.

Rollo May cogently pointed out in his book *Power and Innocence*[2] that all of us need power if we are to function with dignity and self-respect. Stripping people of power is the quickest way to humiliate and degrade them and to promote violence. May observes that violence grows out of a feeling of impotence: when people sense that they no longer have any options, they lash out blindly and irrationally. Thus it is clearly not to a pastor's or church board's self-interest that parishioners be devoid of any kind of power.

Most of us are much more conscious of the power of others than we are of our own power. Within human systems, we are more aware of the power of those in authority over us than we are of the power and authority we have in our relationships with others. Most of us could also be much more powerful within our churches and work settings than we actually are. To more effectively exercise power within a congregation, however, specific principles need to be followed and certain skills mastered. Every member in a parish needs enough power to get what he or she wants.

What needs to be avoided is "poverty mentality"—the belief that if I am to get what I want, others must be robbed of what they want. This scarcity mentality denies the abundance of God's gifts. Abundance thinking affirms that when I empower others, everyone in the system, including me, becomes more powerful. I wish more clergy understood this dynamic. Clergy who tightly hold the reins of ministry eventually disempower laity, who then lose their motivation to stay active and involved. As a result, the energy of the congregation slowly dries up. But the more clergy empower lay people to do the ministry of the congregation, the more powerful they as clergy become. When all members of a system pursue their goals with vigor, the system is infused with energy, and the effective leader helps members to reconcile their personal self-interest with the self-interest of the wider congregation.

Personal Power

Every individual possesses some form of personal power. Rollo May identifies four types.

1. *Self-affirmation* is the confidence people have that they are worthy of the space they occupy on this earth. It is the power to say, "I am a worthwhile human being and I deserve to be here." When one has the power to assert one's own dignity and respect oneself, then one has ample quantities of this type of power.
2. *Self-assertion* is setting firm personal boundaries and refusing to let others transgress these boundaries. The famous statement of Martin Luther, "Here I stand, I can do no other, God help me," is a good example of this type of power.
3. *Aggression* is intruding into someone else's space and rearranging the resources there. All of us possess the potential for aggression and sometimes are unknowingly aggressive, and we need to be in touch with our values about the rights and dignity of others as we think about employing this power.
4. *Violence* is irrationally lashing out when one has a sense that there are no other options. In many ways, it is an act of impotence. Therefore, it is important not to press others to the point where they no longer feel they have integrity or self-respect. People in a congregation who believe they have no power in the system might act out in destructive ways.

Bruce Reed of the Grubb Institute in London, England, identified other forms of personal power.

1. *Instrumental power.* Ever since the first caveman realized he was a more effective fighter with a club in his hand, humans have been developing ways to extend their power. Those who have a bowl in which to carry water possess more power than those without one. Today instrumental power extends to our clothes, cars, computers, cell phones, credit cards, and so forth. Each of us probably has more instrumental power than we realize, since we often take our instruments for granted.

2. *Power of projection.* Each of us elicits projections from others that may or may not be congruent with the self-image we are trying to project. These projections, however, greatly influence the way we are perceived. If people see us as powerful, we do indeed have power with them. If they perceive us as pushovers, they will treat us that way, although we may have more personal power than they know.

3. *Power of position.* This kind of power has more to do with the way we use our positions than with our specific role. Although a church secretary may not carry much role authority within the parish, he or she may effectively use that position—to block certain communications or start rumors, or to support the work of the youth worker or a planning team. Whenever people in a parish elect someone to a position of authority, they try to assess either consciously or unconsciously whether that person will exploit the power of that position.

Corporate Power

In addition to personal power, each of us possesses corporate power derived from organizations within which we have recognition and influence. Unlike our personal power, which we take with us wherever we go, our corporate power is not easily transportable. Our power in our home congregation, for example, cannot be carried with us to a neighboring congregation.

Our corporate power is directly proportional to our ability to influence either positively or negatively the things that are valued by the members of that system. *Currency of power* is the extent to which we are seen by others in the system as able to influence, for good or ill, what the system holds dear. People who understand currencies of power and are able to work effectively with them are able to amass considerable power within systems. Four currencies of power are valued highly by most congregations. I'll give a brief definition of these now and discuss them in greater detail below.

1. *Reputational power* is given to me by an organization because of its past experiences with me. If over the years I have been viewed as wise and caring and as a person with integrity, people tend to listen when I speak.

2. *Coalitional power* is mine when I am perceived to be part of a caucus or group within the larger system. Someone who has always headed up the congregation softball team usually has high credibility on congregational issues among people who play softball with him or her every summer.

3. *Communicational power* is mine when I have access to important information within a system. A former board member who knows when the board meets and how it functions needs only one phone call to get an item on the agenda of the next board meeting. A newcomer who knows little about how decisions are made in the congregation would not be as powerful.

4. *Structural power* is mine when I occupy a role that is part of the official structure of the congregation. Simply being elected to an office in the congregation gives me this kind of power.

Role Authority and Clarity

One definition of authority is role power. Every system assigns specific authority to individuals occupying various roles. They are given enough authority to execute the functions of their roles. The parish in essence says, "You do not need to exercise any personal or corporate power in order to perform these functions; we as a system give you all the authority you need for these tasks." Hence the subtle difference between power and authority. Authority is granted to people by the system through roles. Power relates to individuals' ability to accomplish things beyond the authority given to them in roles.

The degree to which individuals are able to act with authority within their roles is directly proportional to the clarity of their role within the congregation. When there is role confusion (that is, disagreement within the system about the function of a role), the authority of people in the role is undermined. A church school superintendent, for example, may be accustomed to ordering all church school material. During a dispute regarding curriculum, however, the superintendent's authority to carry out that function may be challenged. He may subsequently discover that there was no clear job description and that in the middle of the dispute, the parish Christian education committee decided to usurp that authority. The superintendent may then need to assert whatever personal and corporate power he has in order to perform the functions of the role. The clearer the role becomes, the more authority the person occupying it will have.

Analyzing Power

Power and authority are related because the people who possess clear role authority in a system usually have access to other sources of power within that system. Above I identified several currencies of corporate power:

- coalitional power
- reputational power
- communicational power
- structural power

The first three are forms of informal power. People who have these types of power may exercise them whether or not they hold a certain role. Structural power, on the other hand, is formal power. People only have this power as long as they hold a particular office. Another word for structural power, or role power, is authority, as explained above.

People who hold important roles within a congregation normally have greater access to the other currencies of power. This is why individuals who occupy certain roles within a congregation over many years are so powerful. Often, when they no longer are performing up to congregational expectations, congregational leaders are not able to remove them from office because they possess enormous amounts of informal power within the system. They are well known (reputational power). They have access to many informal groups in the parish (coalitional power). They know most of the people in the congregation and know who to talk to when their position is threatened (communicational power). In addition to this corporate power, they also bring their own personal power to their office.

Congregational leaders need to know who possesses enough informal and corporate power within the congregation to influence the outcome of a decision. It is possible to determine which individuals or groups must support a decision if it is to pass, and the rest of this article demonstrates how to make such a determination. Your ability to identify and understand the operative currencies of power in your congregation will greatly influence how effectively you lead. Once you understand the four currencies, you can begin to use them to accomplish specific goals.

Coalitional Power

Coalitional power is the power a group of like-minded people have within a system. They have the advantage of numbers. When they speak with one voice on an issue, their view holds considerable credibility. Saul Alinsky used to say, "Solo is dodo." For a coalition to exercise power in a system, however, its members need to have similar self-interests or at least the ability to collaborate. Make a list of all the subgroups within your congregation. Include formal groups, such as the choir, the youth group, men's or women's groups; and informal groups, such as the members who bowl together on Tuesday evenings, assemble in the lounge before worship, or head to the local coffee shop after services. Each group probably has a specific, identifiable vested interest or point of view. You could do a power analysis of the congregation using this listing alone. You should be able to tally which of these groups will be for any given issue and which will be against it.

If your congregation is divided into various factions, identify these groups, noting the people who belong to them. For example, there may be liberal, fundamentalist, charismatic, social activist, conservative, and socialite factions. A faction may remain unorganized until a specific issue pulls it together, and it is helpful to determine where members of a faction are united and where they are divided. Because factions may be larger and less unified than a coalition, it may be more difficult to work with them.

Now list the key individuals at the center of each formal and informal group and faction, the people who give primary leadership or whose point of view is most often adopted. These are the people who have coalitional power. Whenever they are upset about something, they have a caucus to which they can bring their concern. When that happens, you are no longer faced with just one upset person: a whole cluster of people is upset.

Reputational Power

Reputational power is held by the people with high credibility in the congregation. A congregation rarely has more than a half-dozen of these people. Some people's credibility originates outside the congregation.

For example, in some congregations, doctors automatically have high credibility. When an issue emerges in the congregation that frightens or confuses members, they turn to see how the people with reputational power are responding. This category includes natural leaders with charisma who have led the parish whenever it was in a tight spot—particularly during a pastoral transition. Also in this category are people who act in unexpected ways, who throw the congregation off base with erratic or bizarre behavior. People will coddle them or give in to them to prevent their "unexpected" behavior from erupting. List all these people.

Communicational Power

Communicational power, also called informational power, is the power both to retrieve accurate information about a system and to disseminate information throughout the system. One can easily see this type of power at work in political elections. A candidate for office has great power if she knows clearly what issues are of concern to people. The candidate's ability to communicate a clear plan for addressing those issues extends her power. The best platform in the world is useless if it fails to address people's real concerns or is never really heard.

Simply being on site can give people informational power. Some people spend a good deal of time at the church, and their very presence gives them access to the information flow of the parish. Parish secretaries, for example, can be very powerful because of the amount and type of information they accumulate. Custodians, church organists, retired people who hang around the church, and certain church officers all may be listed in this category.

Sometimes there is power in inaccurate or distorted information, especially if someone can disseminate distorted information and give it credibility in the system. If, for example, a congregation is debating whether to put in an elevator and someone starts a rumor that installing an elevator would require replacing all electrical wiring of the church, that rumor could scuttle the project.

Trace the various formal and informal communication systems within your parish. Who are the people who control formal communications within the parish? To what extent do others have access to that formal system? How effective is each formal communication link? Now pay attention to the informal communications systems within the parish. Who has whose ear? When a piece of "hot" information is dropped, who gets in touch with whom to talk about it? Who is included in each informal network? Who is left out? Does the information get distorted as it moves through some grapevines? Some groups are interested only in certain kinds of information; others take any data and slant it in a certain direction. The more accurately you are able to determine who operates these networks and how they function, the more communicational or informational power you will have.

Structural Power

Structural power is in the hands of those who occupy formal roles or positions in the congregation. We might say these people have role power or authority. Congregations are structured in such ways that elected or appointed people have authority within certain aspects of congregational life. List the people who hold official power within the system. Include members of your board, committee chairs, choir directors, the Sunday school superintendent, officers of various auxiliaries, and so forth.

Power Analysis Chart

In the chart on the following page, transfer the names of key figures in each category to the following chart. In the columns after each person's name, place an *X* indicating each area of power they possess.

Once you have listed people in all four categories, you can determine their power base rating by counting the number of columns in which each person's name oc-

curs. If, for example, an individual has reputational power, communicational power, and organizational power, you would place a number 3 beside his name in the "power base rating" column. By doing this tally, you can easily determine who the more powerful people are in your parish. These are the folks with whom you must deal, one way or another, on most major issues. Pause here for a moment to ascertain if these really are the most powerful people in your parish. Who is missing?

Now focus on your personal credibility with each of these individuals. On a scale of 1 to 6 (a rating of 1 is low; 6 is high), rate your credibility with each of these individuals. Do you usually get along with each other? Do you hold compatible theological and political positions on issues? Do you have similar aspirations for the congregation? Even if you do not always agree, do you respect one another?

You now have a way to visualize your power within your congregation. More than likely, you have discovered you are more powerful than you thought. You may also have a clearer idea about where you need to do some homework. If your credibility is low with people who have a power base rating of 2 or more, you need to develop trust and understanding with those individuals. What do they want or expect from you and the parish? Where are they invested? Who are the people they listen to? In short, what is their self-interest? To be powerful with these individuals, you need to be seen by them as being able to frustrate or enhance their self-interest. What is your best way of achieving that image?

The power analysis chart can also be used to examine each controversial issue that emerges within the congregation. To do this, instead of rating your personal credibility with each individual, rate where they stand on the issue. (A rating of 1 is extreme opposition; 6 is complete support.) You now can see which people have a high power base rating and must be won over on that particular issue.

Power Analysis Chart

Name of Person	Coalitional Power	Reputational Power	Communicational Power	Structural Power	Power Base Rating	Self-Assessment: My Credibility with This Person
John Doe			X	X	2	1 2 3 4 5 6
						1 2 3 4 5 6
						1 2 3 4 5 6
						1 2 3 4 5 6
						1 2 3 4 5 6
						1 2 3 4 5 6
						1 2 3 4 5 6
						1 2 3 4 5 6
						1 2 3 4 5 6
						1 2 3 4 5 6
						1 2 3 4 5 6
						1 2 3 4 5 6
						1 2 3 4 5 6

You might need to exercise your negotiation skills. Most of us are such incorrigible collaborators but we do not know how to do tough negotiating. Negotiation should take place when collaboration is impossible because individuals' vested interests are incompatible and a contest with them would be too costly. Negotiation takes place when people trade value for value until a reasonable compromise is reached. Letha Scanzoni calls negotiation "mutual submission." The powerful people who oppose your position on the current issue may be invested in others. Maybe you can facilitate their getting some of what they want on those issues if they support you on this issue. To be uncompromising is really to demand either acquiescence or a fight. Either may be costly and in the long run undermine your effectiveness and the welfare of others. *Compromise* is not a bad word or concept. It is all part of being powerful and effective.

If This Does Not Work for You

If this power analysis does not produce clarity and insight into the power dynamics of your congregation, try going back and analyzing in greater depth the subgroups or factions in the congregation that have coalitional power. If your congregation is divided into factions that support specific faith stances or approaches to your faith tradition, do your power analysis along those lines. Who are the people who are at the core of each faction? Rate your credibility and influence with each of those core leaders. Analyze what kind of power each faction has in the parish by noting who in each faction has a role in the decision-making structure of the parish. Are there factions that have a disproportionate amount of power in the congregation, who wield more power than their numbers warrant? Who has been disenfranchised by factions wielding disproportionate amounts of power?

Does one group or another—such as the Sunday school, choir, or a committee—control certain areas of congregational life? If so, this is not necessarily bad. These groups may provide the right kind of energy to keep the congregation moving. But when a group has a stranglehold on a piece of the congregation and people are hurt in the process, you should be concerned. If people with leadership ability get locked out and their function in the congregation suffers, changes need to be made. Every faction in the parish should get enough of what its members need and want in order to sustain members' dignity and self-respect. If all points of view are represented in the official decision-making body of the congregation, decision making will be tough, but one group will not be continually dominated or ignored, and the energy that group's members have to offer the congregation will not be lost.

If your congregation has many subgroups, it is not necessary for you to have control over every subgroup in the congregation in order to be an effective leader. Basically you need two things from each subgroup or faction within your congregation: (1) accurate information on how the subgroup's members think and feel about issues, and (2) that subgroup's willingness to give your viewpoint a fair hearing. This requires that you have the trust and confidence of at least one or two people in that group. If this is not the case, you have some bridge building to do. How can you gain credibility with at least one or two people within each subgroup? The following questions may help you to devise a strategy for relating to each of your congregational groups.

1. What is the specific self-interest of this group? What values do they espouse? On what issues are they likely to become active?

2. How unified is the group? Is it likely to split at certain points? Under what circumstances would this happen?

3. Who is at the core of the group? Who are the spokespersons, the ones who shape the point of view, whose point of view is usually accepted? Who is at the fringes of the group? What keeps them from being part of the "in" group?

4. Where are you with this group—as a group and with each individual within this group? Whose ear do you have in this group? Do you have ways both of feeding information to this group and of remaining informed about their thinking, feeling, and activity?

5. To increase your influence with the group, with what action do you need to begin and with what individuals?

With some work, you should be able to use the special resources of each subgroup in the congregation to further the mission of the congregation. If that is not possible, at least you may be able to minimize the negative effect certain groups might have in the congregation.

Conclusion

Scripture tells us, "Where there is no vision, the people perish." It takes power not only to produce a vision, but also to make that vision a reality. This is the quality of leadership that is called for in congregations today. Clergy first need to negotiate their role to become clear about what authority the congregation wants them to have. This is just a starting point, but clearly it is an important one. If the top leaders in an organization do not assume their rightful authority, others in the system will not be able to assume their authority. The pastor must be a strong leader in worship, crisis ministry, and various other pastoral acts. Congregations also depend on clergy to help them envision and realize possibilities. To carry out their calling, clergy need to be knowledgeable about and at home with the use of power within that congregational system.

George Peabody, creator of the *Peabody Power Game*, a simulation game that helps people understand the dynamics of power, claims that many people see themselves as far less powerful than they really are. Here are some of the reasons he cites for their misperception:

* They ignore the real currencies of power.
* They forget that power is based on the way they are seen by others.

- They hold on to untested fantasies about the power of others ("them").
- They are unaware of their own resources.
- They are unable to see the tactical options available to them, and impotence results.
- They are unable to know how to use all three strategies of power—collaboration, negotiation, and fight—or they feel uncomfortable doing so.
- They are afraid to go after what they want.[3]

I hope the term *power* has been redeemed from negative connotations and that congregations, clergy, and lay leaders will assume the power and authority necessary to be an effective church within a broken world. If you are perceived by others as being powerful, then in fact you are powerful. When people see you as reliable, trustworthy, and likely to act in their best interests, your credibility within the congregation will build and you will accumulate power. If you remain clear about the factor of self-interest and the ends to which you are directing your power, you are on your way to being a powerful person within your congregation. Do not be afraid to use your power. Use it well for God, congregation, and the wider community.

Notes

This article is based on the monograph "Power Analysis of a Congregation" by Roy M. Oswald, copyright © 1981, 2001, 2002 (revised and enlarged edition) by the Alban Institute, Inc. Used by permission.

1. Hans Selye, *Stress Without Distress* (New York: Signet Books, 1975).
2. Rollo May, *Power and Innocence: A Search for the Sources of Violence* (New York: W.W. Norton, 1972).
3. George Peabody and Paul Dietterich, *Powerplay* (Naperville, Ill.: Powerplay, Inc., 1973).

STARTING UP AS A REDEVELOPMENT PASTOR

NOTHING ON EARTH LIVES FOREVER. Instead, life expresses itself in cycles of birth and death, emergence and decline. Congregations manifest similar patterns. A "birth" moment gives way to a period of "formation" (in which congregational identity, purpose, and norms take shape). If the emerging congregation offers a ministry relevant to the surrounding environment, it may attain "stability." Since founding members grow older and community demographics change, the original fit between congregation and context will, at some point, diminish—resulting most often in numerical "decline." Finally, if the decline is unchecked (or if the particular ministry task is finished), the congregation will experience "death."

What Is Redevelopment?

Congregations renew their life and mission by returning to issues typical of the formation period. (Who are we? What are we here for? Who is our neighbor?) Some congregations wait longer than others before they grapple seriously with those questions. The diagram on the next page illustrates three paths back to the formation portion of the life cycle.

This chart shows loops back to the formation stage from three different points in the life cycle: stability (or the first inklings of sagging energy), moderate decline, and advanced decline. Each of these dotted paths has its characteristic dynamics. Let's examine them one at a time.

Ongoing Renewal

In a time when stability is drifting toward stagnation, a congregation might find a way to take a fresh look at the three formation questions. In the evangelical tradition, periodic revivals may have served this purpose to some extent, long before anyone started to study congregational development. In Roman Catholic traditions, teams from religious orders would come to a church and conduct a preaching mission. These periods of intense proclamation, prayer, song, and study would interrupt "business as usual" and press the church back to fundamental questions of faith. Because they were system-wide interventions, they introduced common language and frameworks to which leaders could later refer as church decisions were made. Today it is common for churches to engage in strategic planning—even in times of relative stability—to refocus the congregation on fundamentals and to ask challenging questions about identity, purpose, and context. Other congregations rely on the self-study process

"Renewal, Revitalization, Redevelopment"[1]

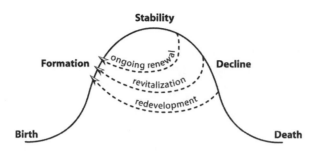

that accompanies the selection of a new pastor to help them take stock.

Two tendencies prevent churches from revisiting the formation questions when everything seems to be working. First, the renewal event, self-study, or planning process may be rejected outright under the banner, "If it ain't broke, don't fix it." The new perspective provided by a revival leader, consultant, or self-study process may seem quite unnecessary, since the congregation's key programs are humming along successfully. Second, the congregation may undertake the process but discount any disturbing trends or hard questions that come to the surface. Some theorists argue that a system will never question its fundamental assumptions until the pain induced by present practices becomes intolerable.

Revitalization

In the early stages of decline, a congregation might gain some motivation to revisit the formation issues. If some way is found to look hard at the facts, avoid blame, and engage in new learning, we might call this process revitalization—a term implying that there is still substantial vitality present that can be refreshed and refocused. Though congregations usually expect that the call (or appointment) of a new pastor

will accomplish this work automatically, a change in leadership will not, by itself, alter the curve. If the new pastor has the skills, information, and political support to raise the formation questions again effectively, a new era of vitality might ensue. More typically, the forces driving the decline—internal dysfunction, external change, or both—will be ignored until things get worse. In that case, the new pastor will experience (and often collude with) the congregation's two most destructive illusions: the fantasy that growth can occur without change, and the fantasy that change can occur without conflict.

Redevelopment

When a congregation has been declining steadily for years and even decades, and has sustained significant losses in people, energy, flexibility, and funds, then the path back to the formation issues is far more costly. The farther you slip down the decline side of the curve, the more capital it takes—spiritually, financially, and politically—to create the possibility of a turnaround. Yet there may still be tremendous potential for spiritual growth, invitational outreach, and community ministry.

In my experience, redevelopment efforts are often "undercapitalized" in three ways. Many are set up for:

1. Spiritual failure: The congregation has not really faced the fact that it is dying—that many (if not most) elements of an old identity and purpose must be relinquished if anything new is to occur.
2. Financial failure: Leaders are working with an inadequate budget or overoptimistic revenue projections.
3. Political stalemate: Leaders—at both the congregational and denominational levels—severely underestimate the amount of political resistance that redevelopment efforts can provoke and the toll it can take on leaders to face that resistance.

Mike Regele has said it well in his book *Death of the Church*: "The Church has a choice: to die as a result of its resistance to change, or to die in order to live."[2]

A New Pastor on the Redevelopment Pathway

Although the dynamics described in the rest of this volume will apply to the redeveloping congregation, some additional challenges face the pastor beginning this type of ministry.

Long, Slow Decline Creates Its Own Psychology

Whatever the causes of decline may have been, certain effects of long decline are predictable. Leaders and members tend to experience some degree of depression, self-doubt, and helplessness. These feelings may be hidden behind optimistic statements ("We are a great little church") or behind the "can do" response a congregation shows when its survival is imminently threatened. Denominational officials and prospective pastors need to pay attention to the undertow of grief and fear in a declining church's psyche.

An incoming pastor should also recognize the dynamic of psychological self-selection that occurs as people join churches. Those most excited about numerical growth and invitational outreach will tend to find their way to growing congregations. A congregation that has been in a survival mode for many years will tend to draw a higher proportion of people who understand themselves as "survivors." These folk may bring deep faith and wonderful personal qualities to the congregation, but they often lack another set of gifts that would be required to generate (or even tolerate) vision, change, conflict, and growth. Survivor personalities may especially value the characteristics of the family-size church and may suffer a terrible sense of loss if the congregation succeeds in changing size.

Human System Factors Have Often Contributed to the Extended Decline

A long, slow decline has usually been driven primarily by "contextual factors"—demographic and economic changes in the neighborhood and region; changes in the reputation or cultural standing of the parent denomination; and changes in the wider culture. However, the congregation's failure to *adapt* effectively to these factors may reflect human system dynamics that will hinder redevelopment. Examples might include:

Inability to "Pass the Mantle" of Leadership from One Generation to the Next. Members of the founding generation or the most recent "glory days" may be holding the reins too tightly to allow younger or newer leaders to undertake needed innovation. Key leaders with long tenure may retain enormous influence without holding any official position on the search committee or the church board. As a result, covenants are sometimes worked out between official bodies and a new pastor with no engagement of the congregation's longstanding power structure. Informal influencers may not even pay much attention to such negotiations, because they know that they have been able to stop any "unwise" initiatives in the past. The result is an unhappy surprise for both the new pastor and the hard-working committee members, who find themselves blind-sided by opposition when it comes time to implement the agreement.

Patterns of Emotional, Physical, or Sexual Abuse.
Some congregations have declined in part because they have proven to be "unsafe" environments. Perhaps healthier newcomers tend to back away. Perhaps some more vulnerable members have left because they experienced a form of abuse or betrayal. The most common forms of emotional abuse often go unnamed: verbal attacks by one or two members on pastors or lay leaders; "grapevine" criticism; and habits of manipulation—especially threats to withhold a pledge or bequest if the giver does not get his way. Listen carefully for phrases like: "Don't take it personally, that's just Harry (or Sally)." To me, such language signals an inability to hold people accountable for the injurious *effects* of their behavior—regardless of their intentions or their other contributions to parish life.

Excessive Dependence on Clergy (or Denominational Leaders) to "Fix" the Decline.
For many congregations, the only familiar strategy of renewal is to replace the clergy—since pastoral transition times are the only moments when they undertake self-study or goal setting. This pattern can both reflect and produce two assumptions that will undermine redevelopment: namely, it is the pastor's job to get the church growing again, and if things are going wrong, it must be the pastor's fault. Newer and younger clergy are especially vulnerable to the messianic expectations of churches in this pattern. At the beginning, the pastor may be hailed as the "savior." As conflict emerges, the pastor may be cast as the "persecutor" and the congregation as the "victim." (The same dynamic, sometimes called the "rescue triangle" by practitioners of transactional analysis, may also apply in the congregation's relationship with the denomination.)

In at least one denominational body (the Southeastern Pennsylvania Synod of the Evangelical Lutheran Church in America),

the covenant for redeveloping congregations addresses human system dynamics like these. A congregation applying for assistance with redevelopment will undergo (and help pay for) a human systems assessment *before* a redevelopment pastor is sent in, so that patterns like the ones I have described are named and addressed right at the outset. Churches that do not face up to such dynamics are not selected as redevelopment sites. (Further description of this denominational selection process may be found in chapter 5 of *Can Our Church Live? Redeveloping Congregations in Decline,* in the section "A Comprehensive Denominational Strategy.")

The Congregation or the Pastor Has Unrealistic Expectations about the Pace and the Costs of Redevelopment Ministry.
I have already noted the "savior" syndrome—one common expression of unrealistic expectations. Other expressions include:

- Three-year turnaround plans (redevelopment is apt to take seven or more years of persistent and skilled effort).
- Reliance on the pastor's age or family status to create the change. ("If only we had a young couple with small children to draw young families.")
- Insisting that every existing member must be happy with every change. ("We're so small; we can't afford to lose a single member.")
- Trying to be all things to all people. ("Oh, no, we couldn't possibly 'target' any population—we're open to everybody.")

The congregations with the best prospect for redevelopment have engaged in a significant learning process before they make the commitment and have "counted the cost" before they begin.

How a Redevelopment Pastor Can Start Up Well

A new pastor cannot—single-handedly—create the conditions for effective redevelopment ministry. Recognizing the magnitude of the challenge is the beginning of wisdom. Even with effective leadership and a congregation committed to learning, there is no guarantee the project will result in a new era of organizational viability, because the contextual factors driving decline are often very powerful. Somehow, redevelopment pastors have to find a way to give it their best, find joy in the journey, and know deep down that they are loved by God even in the face of apparent failure. There are some things the pastor can do, however, to give the work a fighting chance of success.

- Educate yourself about redevelopment ministry before you accept the call. Visit some congregations that have achieved a turnaround. Interview leaders about the learning steps and conflicts they experienced along the way. Avoid focusing too much on the "model" of ministry they may have discovered; that model may have worked mainly because it fit their context. Focus instead on the way they learned together and the way they handled resistance, conflict, and apparent failure. Also, speak with several denominational leaders who have extensive experience with redevelopment work.

- Educate yourself about this particular congregation before you accept the call. Speak with neighboring clergy about the church's reputation, dynamics, and history. Speak with former pastors. Speak with the denominational leaders most likely to know where the "bodies are buried" (this may not be the staff person currently partnering with the congregation on its call process). Between the time you are issued a call and the time you say yes, make a visit to the church on a day when you can sit down with appropriate leaders to look at the attendance record books, the financial books, and the accounting procedures. Interview all current church employees, with careful attention to any employees who may also be members.

- Negotiate the basic conditions for a redevelopment ministry before you accept the call, and involve an appropriate third party in that negotiation. You are at a great advantage if there is an experienced denominational official helping to build a covenant between denominational office, pastor, and lay leadership. Here is what that covenant looks like in the Southeastern Pennsylvania Synod.

PREAMBLE: As the redevelopment of this congregation begins, it is essential that the partnership and the accountability structure be clearly understood by all parties.

The active participants are the CONGREGATION (represented by the church council), SYNOD (through the bishop, staff person, and mission director), and the PASTOR/REDEVELOPER.

PART ONE—Term of the Call and Subsequent Call

The call to serve as pastor/redeveloper of this congregation comes from the Synod Council of the Southeastern Pennsylvania Synod of the ELCA (with the advice and consent of the congregation). The call is extended for a term of three years. During the term of the call the synod will conduct annual ministry reviews with the pastor and the congregation council. At the conclusion of third year of the term call, with the consent of the bishop, the pastor, and the congregation council, the pastor/redeveloper may be called by the congregation to serve as pastor.

PART TWO—Basic Expectations of the Pastor

- The primary role of the pastor/redeveloper (in addition to being preacher/teacher and spiritual leader) is that of evangelist. It is expected that 50 percent of the pastor's time will be dedicated to the task of evangelization, which includes both visitation, incorporation, faith formation for the new Christians, and training of the laity for the shared task of evangelization.

- The pastor/redeveloper and lay leaders are to participate in a minimum of two Evangelization Conferences during the three-year term.
- The pastor/redeveloper will be responsible for the following:
  a. cultivating a hospitable climate for growth;
  b. making creative use of worship services for the purpose of inviting new members to the congregation, and adding services as needed to maximize outreach;
  c. developing, in consultation with the mission director and the council, a five-year vision for church growth with significant increase in worship attendance;
  d. filing reports with the mission director and the congregation council.

PART THREE—Basic Expectations of the Congregation

The congregation has committed itself to a program of intentional growth in worship attendance and financial support. With the clear understanding that 50 percent of the pastor's time will be given to the task of evangelization, the members of the congregation will be partners with the pastor/redeveloper in this new ministry. That partnership is expressed by a commitment to:

a. provide adequate salary and benefits to the pastor and family;
b. relieve the pastor of excessive committee meetings with the exception of the regular monthly council meetings, and other significant meetings as determined by the laity and clergy leadership;
c. provide specific prayer, support, and programs that directly encourage the work of evangelization;
d. provide for the routine administrative tasks of the congregation;
e. change the existing ministries and programs as suggested by the pastor/redeveloper in order that redevelopment of the mission of the congregation can take place;
f. provide quarterly reports from the president of the congregation council;
g. review and, if necessary, revise the present mission statement of the congregation;
h. share in visitation of the prospective new members identified by the pastor and congregational members;
i. in conjunction with the pastor, develop a five-year vision for church growth.

PART FOUR—Basic Expectations of the Synod

The synod commits itself and its resources to supporting the congregation's redevelopment efforts through the following:

a. Identify, screen, interview, and recommend pastors to serve as pastor/redeveloper. Persons so identified and recommended will have the gifts, skills, and proven experience in revitalizing and redeveloping congregations.
b. Assisting congregations as needed with financial support to the extent available to the synod to enable redevelopment.
c. Mission director will meet at least quarterly with the pastor/redeveloper.
d. Conduct an annual review with pastor and congregation council.

PART FIVE—The Support of the Pastor and Family

As noted above, it is the responsibility of the congregation to provide adequate and just compensation to the person serving as PASTOR/REDEVELOPER of this congregation. Therefore, attached to this agreement is a four-year budget projection indicating the extent of the financial support given to the pastor's compensation package.

Also attached to this agreement are the statements of salary, allowances, and benefits proposed for the initial year of the term call.

_____	_____
Bishop	Congregation Council President
_____	_____
Mission Director	Pastor/Redeveloper

_____
Date

If you do not have a denominational partner to work with in this process, look for a consultant familiar with church redevelopment situations to assist in the negotiation of expectations and to help you with annual reviews of progress. If you do not have another good source of referral, the Alban Institute may be able to recommend someone you could work with. When such a person has been part of the relationship from the start, it is far easier to bring them back for scheduled assessments and for troubleshooting along the way. Believe me, you will need a mutually trusted partner when change issues "hit the fan."

- Include in the written agreement some examples of the kinds of changes that may be needed in order for this church to turn around its decline. Your agreement might say something like this:

We recognize that a congregation that has been declining for a long time will probably need to make some significant changes if it is to grow. Such changes might include (but not be limited to) starting an additional worship service targeted to a particular population in our surrounding community; adjusting the Sunday morning schedule; forming new kinds of groups for spiritual growth and study; and continued learning about redevelopment methods by our board, committees, and other leaders. [You might specify a book you would like them to read together.] We recognize that the needed changes are likely to stir some controversy, so we commit ourselves to learn new ways to handle difference and disagreement. [You might specify a one-day leadership workshop on this subject in the first year, led by a capable third party.]

The purpose here is not to predict everything that will be needed, but rather, to give leaders some concrete idea of what the process may require. Discussing specific examples will help you to assess their dynamics, gauge their level of reactivity to change, and test their capacity for collaborating with clergy.

Before a Pastor Says Yes

I am sure you have noticed that all four of these suggestions have to do with the initial negotiation with the congregation. Other resources in this book will provide you with relevant guidance about building relationships in the first year. But for redevelopment ministries in particular, the quality of the initial negotiation may make or break the subsequent effort. Laying the realities of redevelopment on the table is a profound ministry to the congregation—even if leaders get irritated with you and decide not to call you as pastor. If you shrink from candor and assertiveness in the negotiation, you will have a hard time setting the pattern later. If leaders are offended by straight talk, structured learning, or third-party help, you will want to know that sooner rather than later. Redevelopment ministry is not for the faint-hearted.

I'll offer one final suggestion. Find and use a mentor throughout the redevelopment process. Redevelopment ministry is full of opportunities for spiritual and personal growth, but it can also be lonely, frustrating, and depleting. Make sure you have a place to "go apart" for a while, to experience God's grace through the ministry of a wise companion, reflect on what is happening inside you, and pray about this ministry.

Notes

This article was written by Alice Mann. Used by permission.

1. Alice Mann, *Can Our Church Live? Redeveloping Congregations in Decline* (Bethesda, Md.: The Alban Institute, 1999), p. 9.

2. Mike Regele with Mark Schulz, *Death of the Church* (Grand Rapids: Zondervan Publishing House, 1995).